Coding for Beginners Using PYTHON

Textbook

7

Sangita Chadha

www.bpbonline.com

FIRST EDITION 2022

REPRINT 2023

ISBN: 978-93-5551-226-0

LIMITS OF LIABILITY AND DISCLAIMER OF WARRANTY

The information contained in this book is true to correct and the best of author's and publisher's knowledge. The author has made every effort to ensure the accuracy of these publications, but publisher cannot be held responsible for any loss or damage arising from any information in this book.

All trademarks referred to in the book are acknowledged as properties of their respective owners but BPB Publications cannot guarantee the accuracy of this information.

CBSE is in no way connected with this book. This Book is written solely for the benefit and guidance of students appearing of CBSE Examination.

Distributors:

BPB PUBLICATIONS
20, Ansari Road, Darya Ganj
New Delhi-110002
Ph: 23254990/23254991

MICRO MEDIA
Shop No. 5, Mahendra Chambers,
150 DN Rd. Next to Capital Cinema,
V.T. (C.S.T.) Station, MUMBAI-400 001
Ph: 22078296/22078297

DECCAN AGENCIES
4-3-329, Bank Street,
Hyderabad-500195
Ph: 24756967/24756400

BPB BOOK CENTRE
376 Old Lajpat Rai Market,
Delhi-110006
Ph: 23861747

To View Complete BPB Publications Catalogue Scan the QR Code:

Published by Manish Jain for BPB Publications, 20 Ansari Road, Darya Ganj, New Delhi-110002 and Printed by him at Manipal Technologies Limited, Manipal

www.bpbonline.com

Dedicated to

My children and students

About the Author

Sangita Chadha has been working as Head of Computer Department in Ambience Public School, Safdarjung Enclave, New Delhi from last 15 years. She has over twenty years of experience in the field of education; teaching Computer Science, Informatics Practices and Multimedia & Web Technology to grades XI and XII; and has been multifold responsibilities at her school (Result In-charge, ERP, Website, Almanac, Magazine). She is a passionate learner and committed educator consistently working to make learning enjoyable for the learners. Her foremost classroom pedagogy is centered around project-based learning. She has conducted ICT and Net safety workshops for all stakeholders. She has been part of the curriculum development team for classes IX and X Information and Communication Technology, NCERT. She has co-authored class IX and X ICT for NCERT. She also co-authored Class XII Informatics Practices and Computer Science, NCERT. She has conducted Teacher Training workshops for SCERT Teachers.

Acknowledgements

I would like to acknowledge the contributions of all the educators, data scientists, scientists, and professionals from various fields for their valuable suggestions in developing the content for this book.

I would like to express my gratitude to everyone at BPB Publications for giving us this opportunity to write the book. I am thankful to all the resource persons at BPB Publications for editing, technical reviewing and language editing the book.

I am thankful to my family for being supportive in numerous ways and for giving their unconditional love and support at all times.

Lastly, but not the least, I would like to thank God for bearing me with courage and humility to be able to write this book for our students.

Preface

The primary objective in the development of this book series is to create a fun learning and project-based approach to learn to code. With the help of this, the student will be able to understand, identify and apply the fundamentals of a programming language. It also builds problem-solving skills.

Book will bring an innovative approach among students by Project-based learning which fosters creativity, critical thinking, and innovative ideas that enable a deeper understanding of concepts which leads to longer retention.

The students will start with the approach of looking at the application first and then follow the steps to build an application.

Contents

Installation Guide

Visual Studio Code can be used as an excellent editor for many languages with the help of extensions. It is simple, easy, fun, small in size, and productive. The extensions available make it an excellent editor and are operating system independent.

Students are required to go through the following links to download and install the Python interpreter and then download and install the Visual Studio Code.

Follow the instructions while using the links given below as per your operating system to install Python and Visual Studio Code:

- Python on Linux:

  https://www.python.org/downloads/source/

- Visual Studio Code on Linux:

  https://code.visualstudio.com/docs/setup/linux

- Python on macOS:

  https://www.python.org/downloads/mac-osx/

- Visual Studio Code on macOS:

  https://code.visualstudio.com/docs/setup/mac

- Python on Windows:

  https://www.python.org/downloads/windows/

- Visual Studio Code on Windows:

  https://code.visualstudio.com/docs/setup/windows

- Check out the following links to know more about the Visual Studio code:

  https://code.visualstudio.com/docs

  https://code.visualstudio.com/docs/getstarted/tips-and-tricks

Introduction to Python, Turtle and Visual Studio Code

Structure

In this chapter, you will learn and practice the following concepts:

- Output statement
- Input statement
- Variable
- Operators
  - Arithmetic operators
  - Relational operators
  - Logical operators

Learning Objective

At the end of this chapter, you will be able to:

- Solve simple mathematical problems using input, output, and arithmetic operators
- Create a **Project:** Calculator

- Python is a most popular, high-level, and open-source programming language.
- It is a powerful, fast, interactive, object-oriented, and dynamic programming language.
- It is easy to learn and can run on any platform.
- It is a case-sensitive language. That means uppercase and lowercase letters are not treated the same.

Steps to use Visual Studio Code

- Open Visual Studio Code – Click on the Windows key and type in Visual Studio Code. Click on Visual Studio Code to open the application.

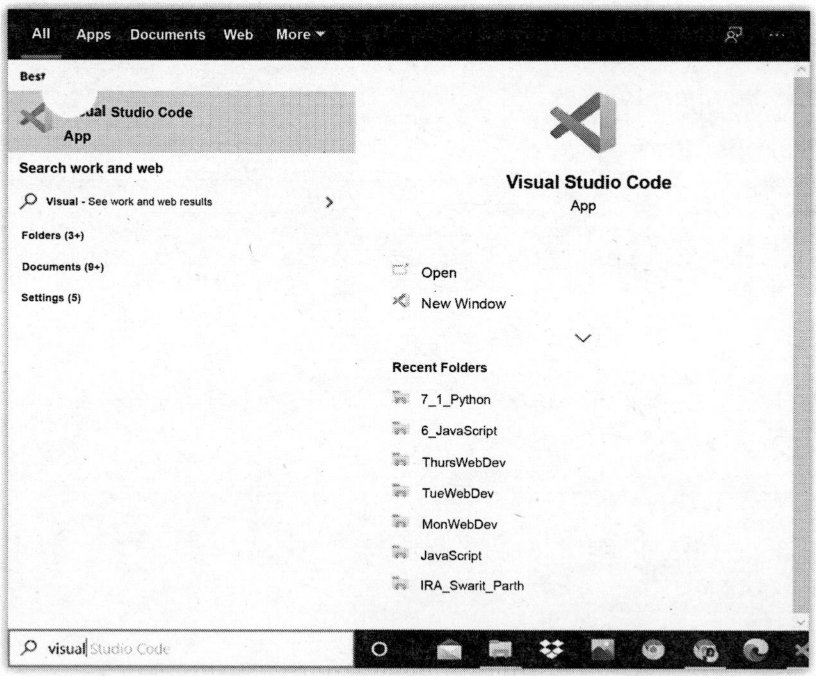

Figure 1.1: Opening of Visual Studio Code

- The Visual Studio Code application looks like as shown in figure 1.2.

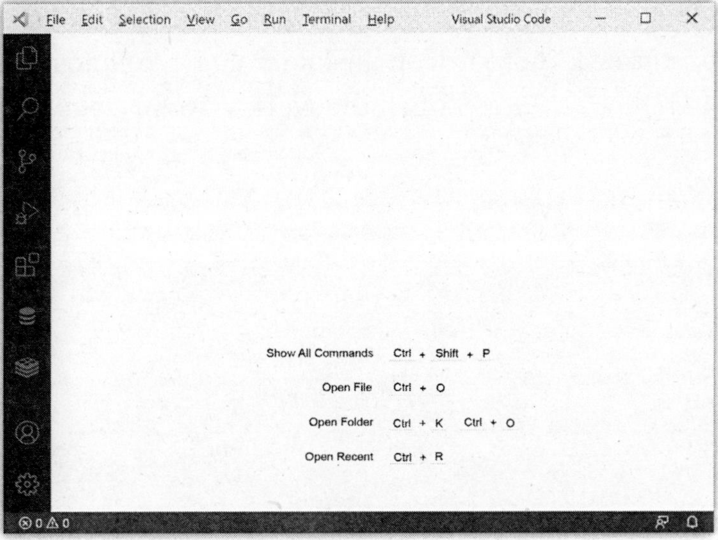

Figure 1.2: Visual Studio Code window

- Now, let us open the folder (i.e. the work area) to place all the python files in that folder. Click on File Open Folder as shown in figure 1.3(a) and then choose the folder to work with.

  For first-time users, a new folder needs to be created.

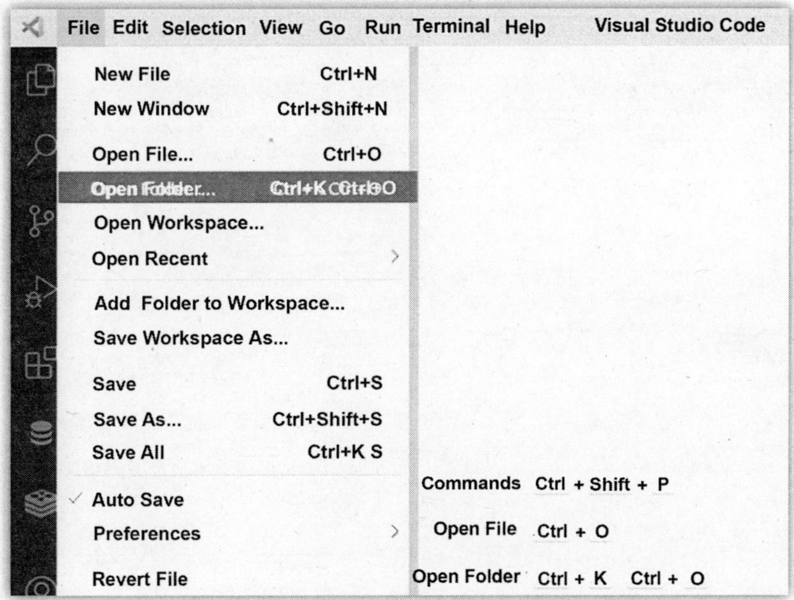

Figure 1.3(a): Open Folder

Choose the path, click on New Folder, and give a name to the folder as shown in *figure 1.3(b)* (For first-time users). Then click on the folder name to choose it and click on Select Folder as shown in *figure 1.3(c)* will open the work area for your python files in Visual Studio Code.

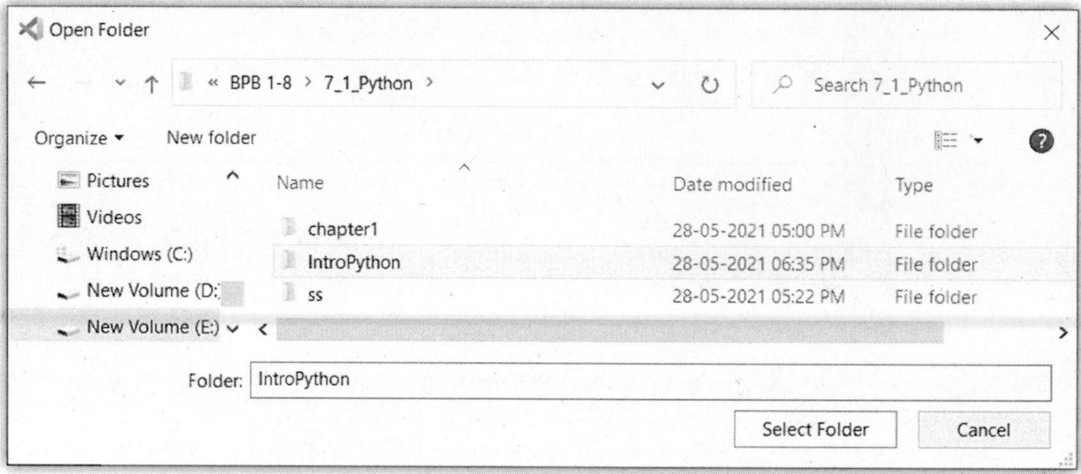

Figure 1.3(b): *Write the filename and put the extension .py*

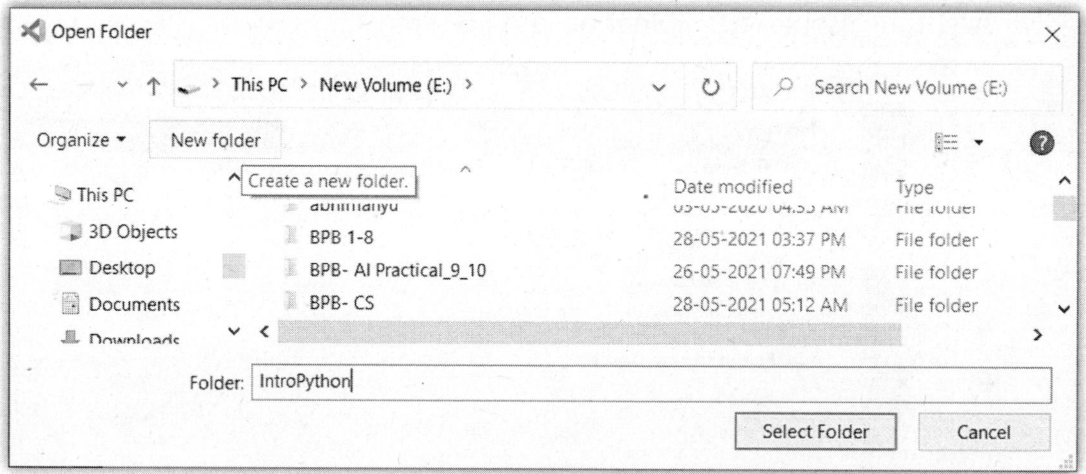

Figure 1.3(c): *Click on this icon to create a new file*

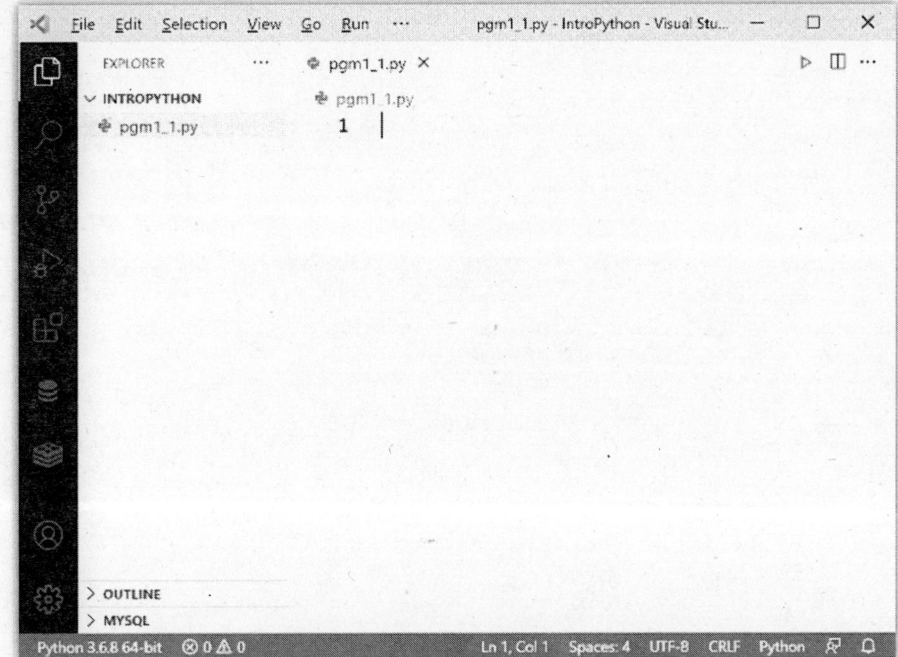

Figure 1.3(d): Terminal Window to display the output of the code

Code Editor Window

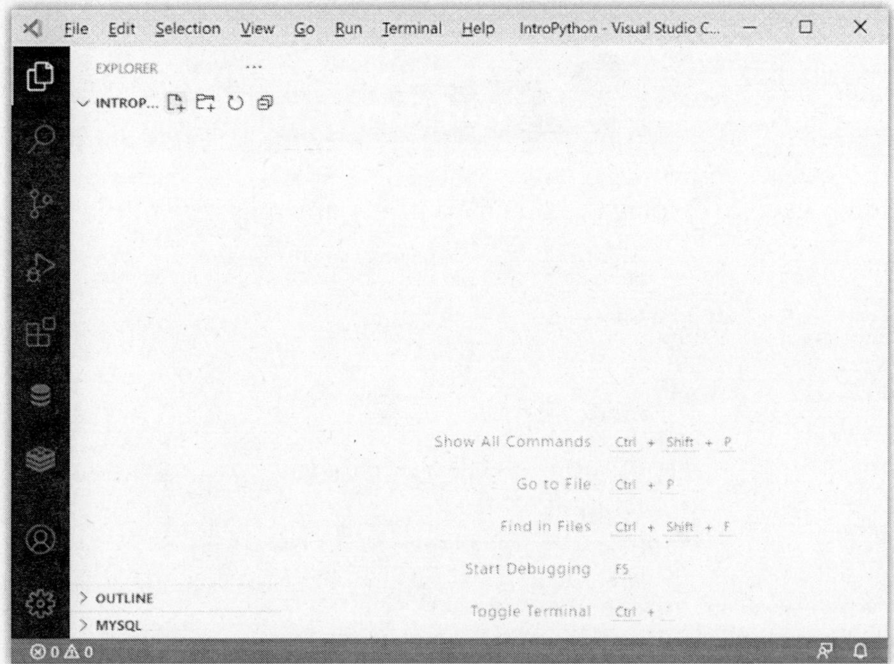

Figure 1.3(e): Click on this icon to execute the code

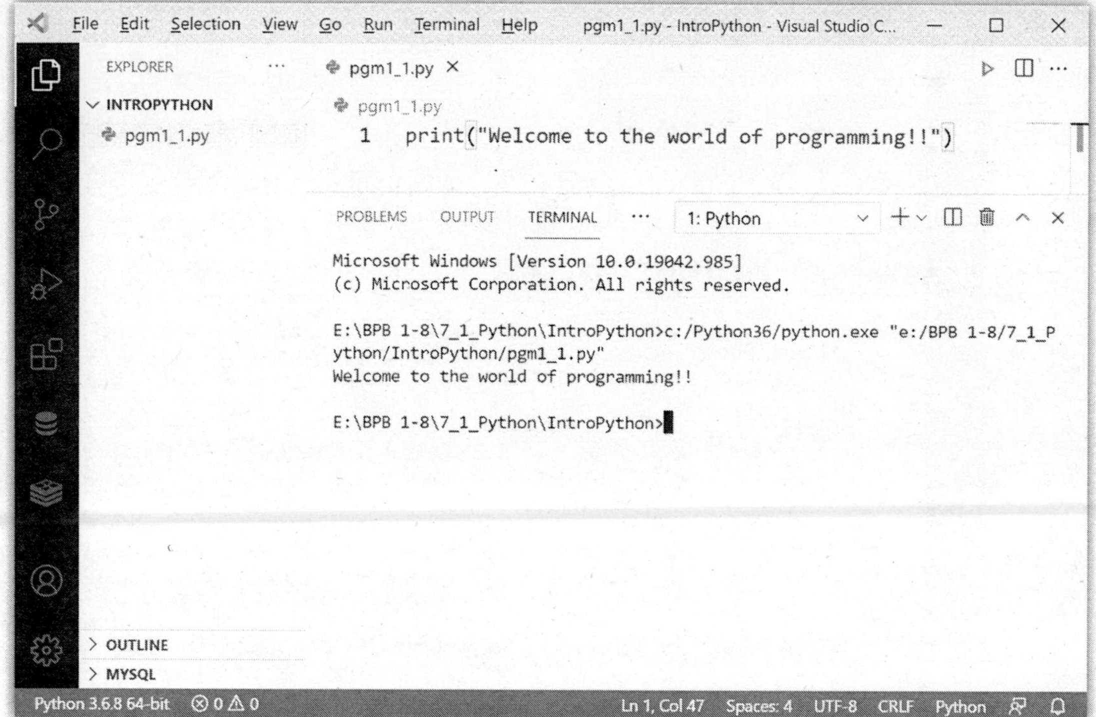

Figure 1.4: Visual Studio Code window

Print function is used to display the result/ output/ any message to the screen.

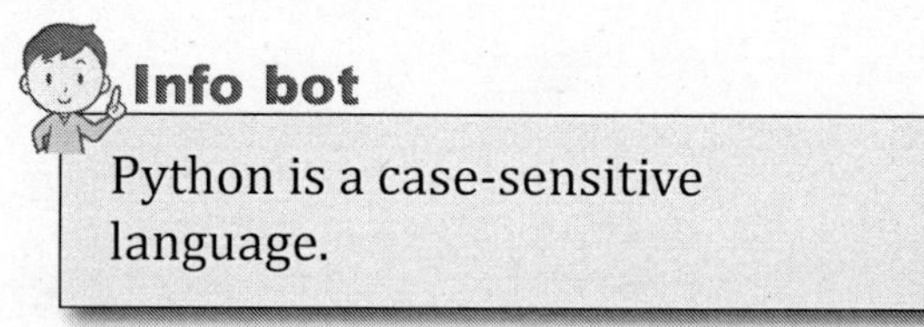

Activity 1.1 Welcome to the world of programming

This program prints the message "Welcome to the world of programming" as shown in figure 1.5.

Output in the Terminal window

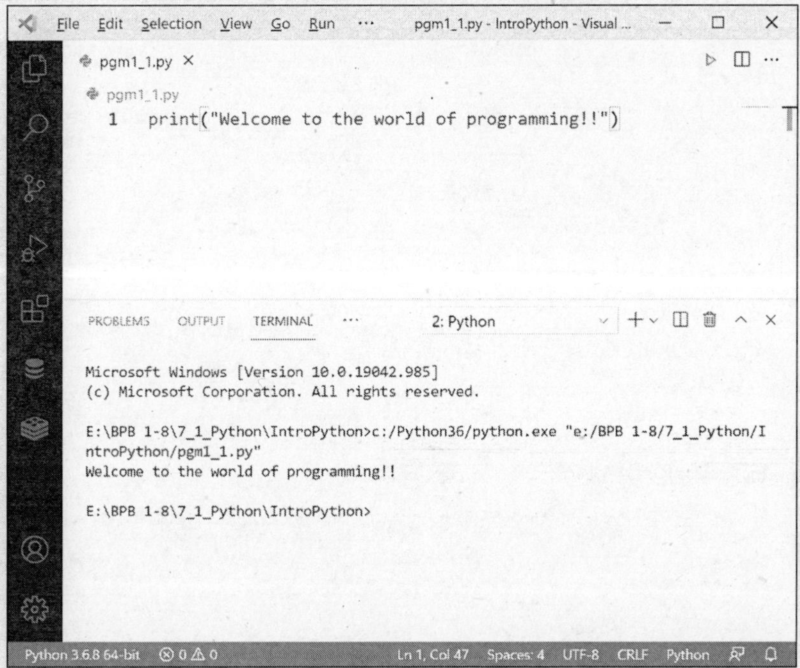

Figure 1.5: Program to display the use of the print statement

Activity 1.2 Perform arithmetic operations (+ and -) on two numbers.

To begin writing the code for the activity given, we require:

- Two variables for numbers [INPUT].
- Two variables for calculating the addition and subtraction operations along with the operators used on the input variable [PROCESS].
- Display the result [OUTPUT].

Info bot

Follow the Input-Process-Output approach to write any program.

Format the output by prefixing the string by using the letter f as shown in figure 1.6. This provides a convenient way to embed python expressions, and variables inside the string using curly brackets {}.

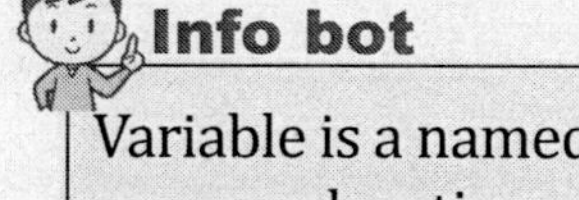

Variable is a named memory location.

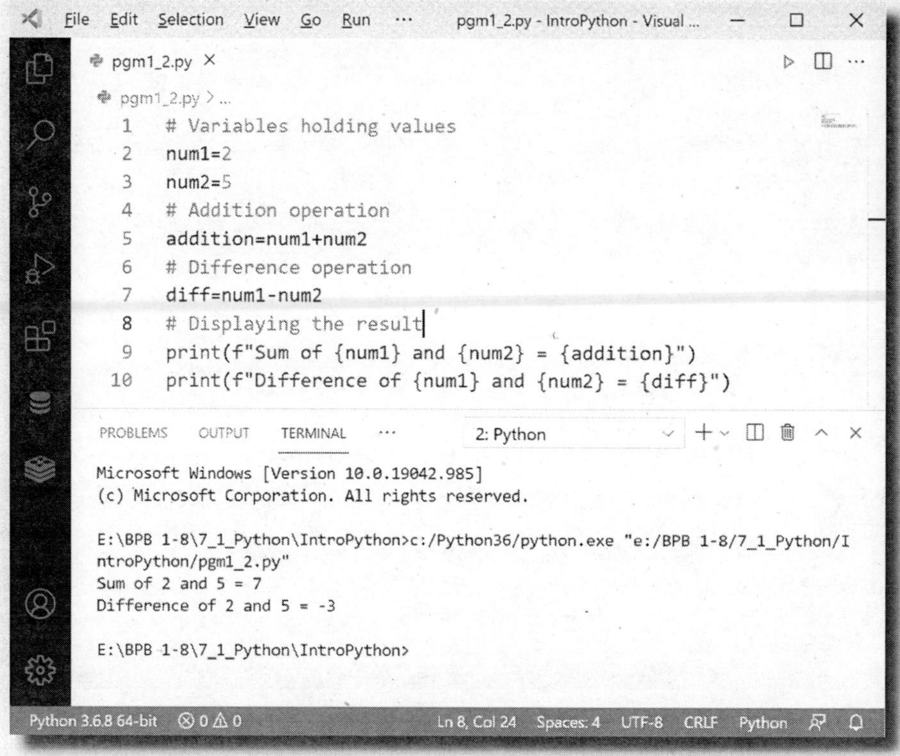

Figure 1.6: Program to perform addition and subtraction

Random module chapter to have the bullet points

- randint
- randrange

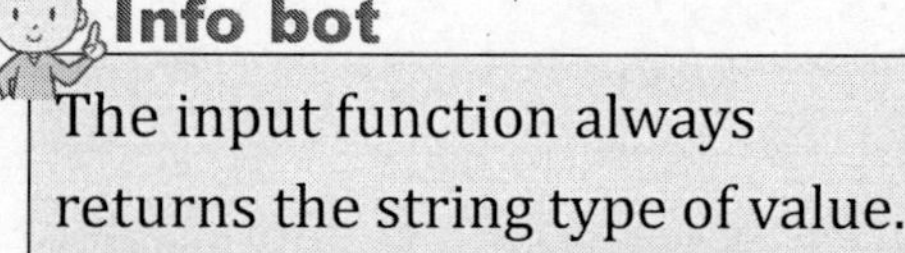

Now the problem with this code is that the user will always get the same output and if the user wishes to change the values of operations, then it requires to open the code and change values. We should be asking the user to provide the input values for operations. To do this, we will need the input() function.

The Input function is used to accept values from the user during run time.

To accept numbers, use **int()** function or **float()** function beforethe input **function()**

The use of the input function with **int()** function is shown in *figure 1.7* to solve Project Calculator.

Info bot

int() returns the integer part of the number, and float() returns the decimal number.

Activity 1.3 Project: Calculator

The calculator which we are creating, performs all the arithmetic operations (+, -, *, /, //, %, **) on two numbers provided by the user.

Figure 1.7: Program Activity 1.3

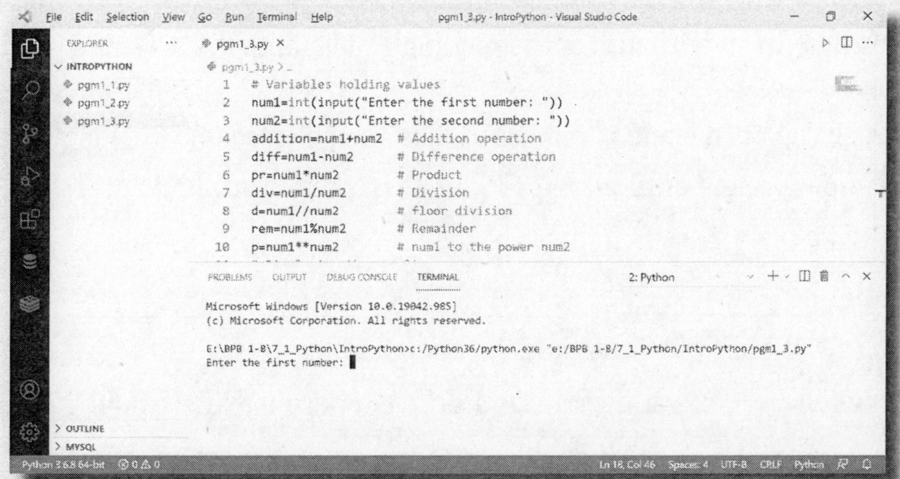

Figure 1.7(a): The output window waits for the user to provide input

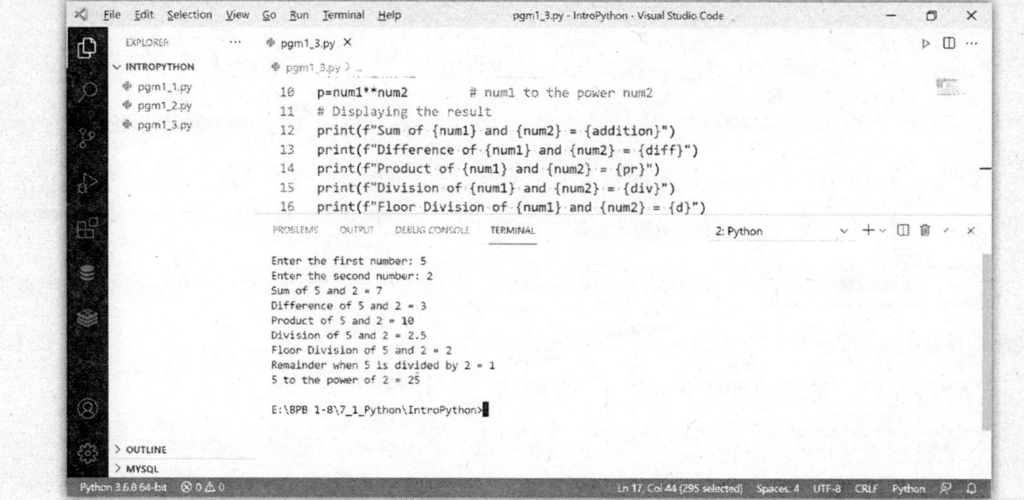

Figure 1.7(b): The output window to show the result for the code

Info bot

Comments are remarks written for the readability and understandability of the code. It begins with a # (hash) symbol in Python and the interpreter doesn't check any errors in the comments.

Practice Questions:

- Read the side of the square. Calculate the area and perimeter of the square.
- Read the radius of the circle. Calculate the area and perimeter of the circle.
- Read the length and breadth of the rectangle. Calculate the area and perimeter of the rectangle.
- Read the weight of an item in milligrams and then display it in the following format:

  For example, weight entered is 2245 mg then the output will be:

  2 KG 2 g 45 mg

Info bot

- **Area of square** = side*side and Perimeter of square=4* side.
- **Area of circle** = PI*radius*radius and circumference of circle=2*PI*radius.
- **Area of rectangle** = Length*Breadth and Perimeter of rectangle=2*(Length + Breadth).

Making Decision

In this chapter, you will learn and practice the following concepts:

- Conditions
  - If
  - If – else
  - If – elif – elif - else
- Operators
  - Relational operators
  - Logical operators
  - Assignment operators
- While loop

Learning Objective

At the end of this chapter, you will be able:

- To build code with decision making
- To build menu-driven code

PROJECT

Menu-Driven Calculator

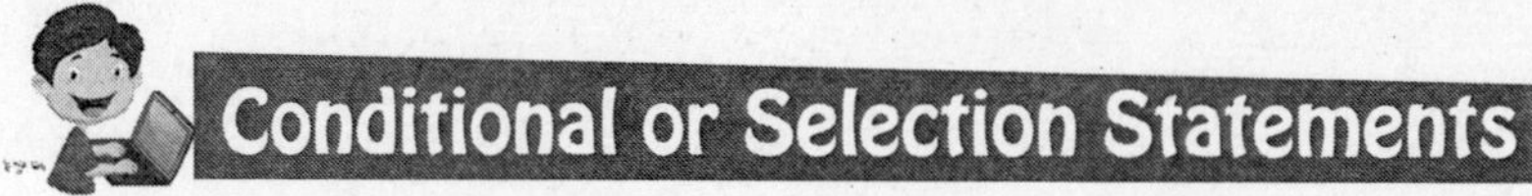

Conditional or Selection Statements

The conditional statement helps in making decisions and branching the flow of control by giving options to choose different paths depending upon some conditions.

The different selection statements are:

- if statement
- if..else statement
- nested if statement
- if..elif..else statement

Info bot

Relational operators (>, <, = =, !=, >=, <=) are used to compare the values. It returns either True or False according to the condition.

Activity 2.1

Read the name of the user and age to check the eligibility for creating an email account. The eligibility criteria for opening an email account is more than 13 years.

File Edit Selection View Go Run ··· pgm2_1.py - IntroPython - Visual S...

pgm2_1.py

```
# Checking Age Eligibility
name=input("Enter your name: ")
age=int(input("Enter your age: "))
if(age>13):
    print(f"Congratulations {name}, you are eligible ")
else:
    print(f"Sorry {name}, you are not eligbilble")
```

Python 3.6.8 64-bit ⊗ 0 ⚠ 0 Ln 8, Col 1 Spaces: 4 UTF-8 CRLF Python

Figure 2.1(a): Code window for Activity 2.1

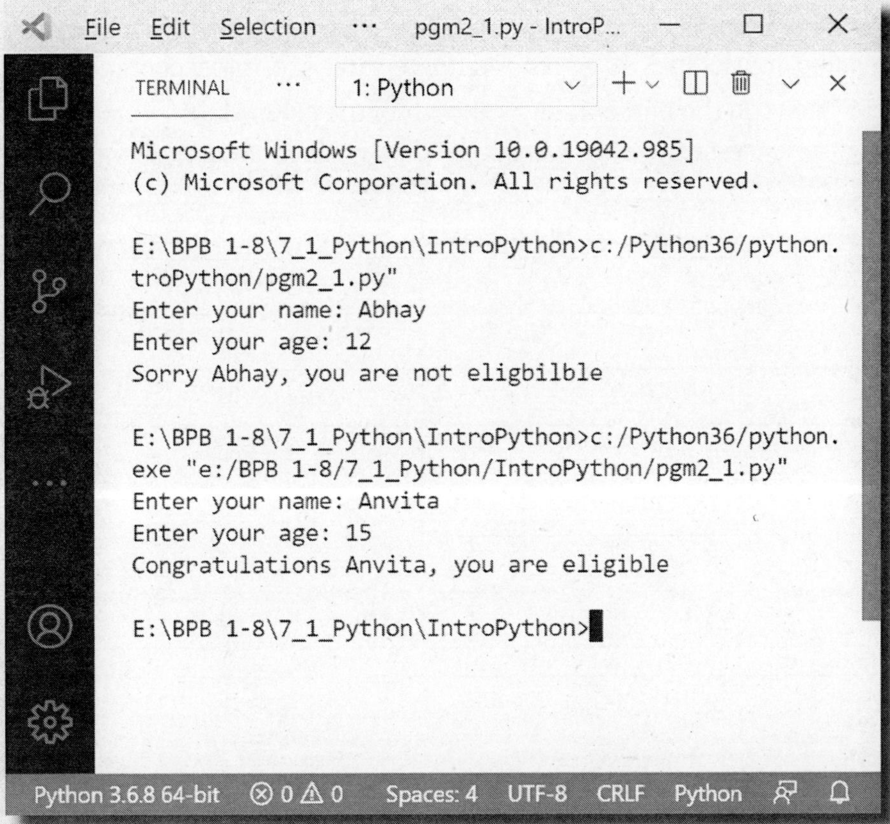

```
File  Edit  Selection  ...  pgm2_1.py - IntroP...
TERMINAL  ...  1: Python

Microsoft Windows [Version 10.0.19042.985]
(c) Microsoft Corporation. All rights reserved.

E:\BPB 1-8\7_1_Python\IntroPython>c:/Python36/python.
troPython/pgm2_1.py"
Enter your name: Abhay
Enter your age: 12
Sorry Abhay, you are not eligbilble

E:\BPB 1-8\7_1_Python\IntroPython>c:/Python36/python.
exe "e:/BPB 1-8/7_1_Python/IntroPython/pgm2_1.py"
Enter your name: Anvita
Enter your age: 15
Congratulations Anvita, you are eligible

E:\BPB 1-8\7_1_Python\IntroPython>

Python 3.6.8 64-bit  ⊗ 0 ⚠ 0  Spaces: 4  UTF-8  CRLF  Python
```

Figure 2.1(b): Output window for Activity 2.1

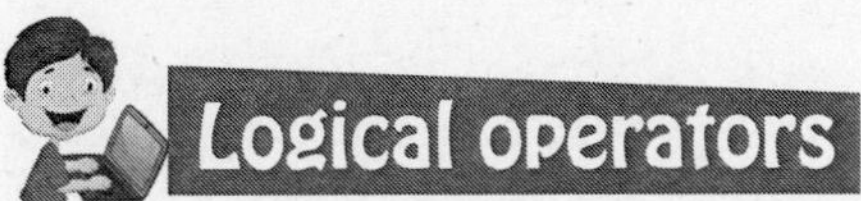

Logical operators are used in combining more than one conditional statement.

- **Logical OR** returns True if any of the conditional statements evaluate to True. It returns False if all the conditional statements evaluate to False.
- **Logical AND** returns True if all the conditional statements evaluate to True. It returns False if any of the conditional statements evaluate to False.

Info bot

Assignment operators are =, + =, - =, * =, / =.

Assignment operators are used in assigning values to variables.

Activity 2.2

Read names and marks in 5 subjects. Calculate total score, percentage and grade. The grade is dependent on the percentage as shown in the given slab:

Percentage	Grade
91 – 100	A1
81 – 90	A2
71 – 80	B1
61 – 70	B2
51 – 60	C1
41 – 50	C2
33 – 40	D
<33	E

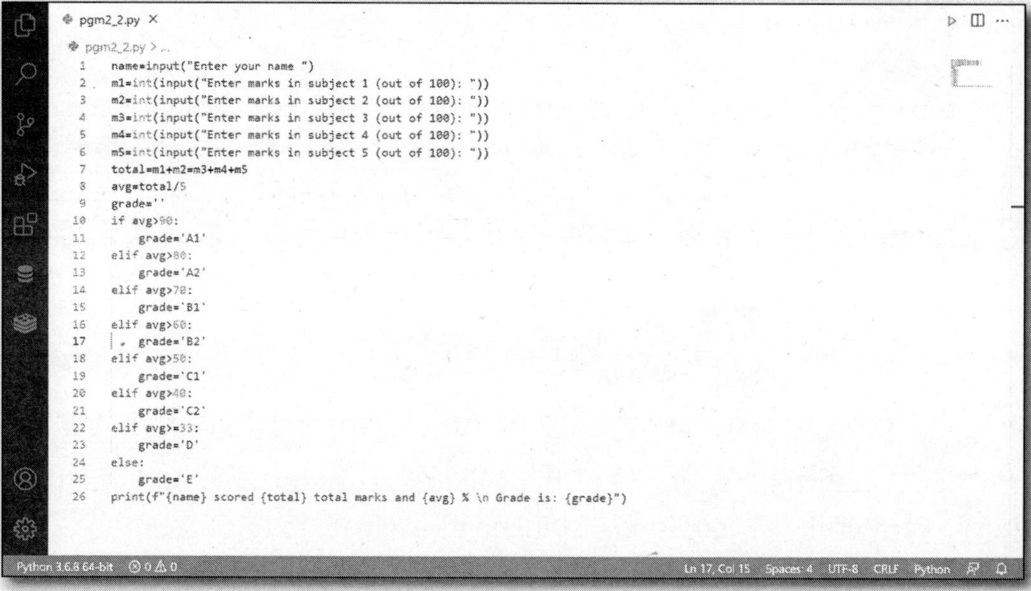

```
name=input("Enter your name ")
m1=int(input("Enter marks in subject 1 (out of 100): "))
m2=int(input("Enter marks in subject 2 (out of 100): "))
m3=int(input("Enter marks in subject 3 (out of 100): "))
m4=int(input("Enter marks in subject 4 (out of 100): "))
m5=int(input("Enter marks in subject 5 (out of 100): "))
total=m1+m2=m3+m4+m5
avg=total/5
grade=''
if avg>90:
    grade='A1'
elif avg>80:
    grade='A2'
elif avg>70:
    grade='B1'
elif avg>60:
    grade='B2'
elif avg>50:
    grade='C1'
elif avg>40:
    grade='C2'
elif avg>=33:
    grade='D'
else:
    grade='E'
print(f"{name} scored {total} total marks and {avg} % \n Grade is: {grade}")
```


Figure 2.2 (a): Code window for Activity 2.2

Info bot

\n is an escape sequence and is used as a newline character.

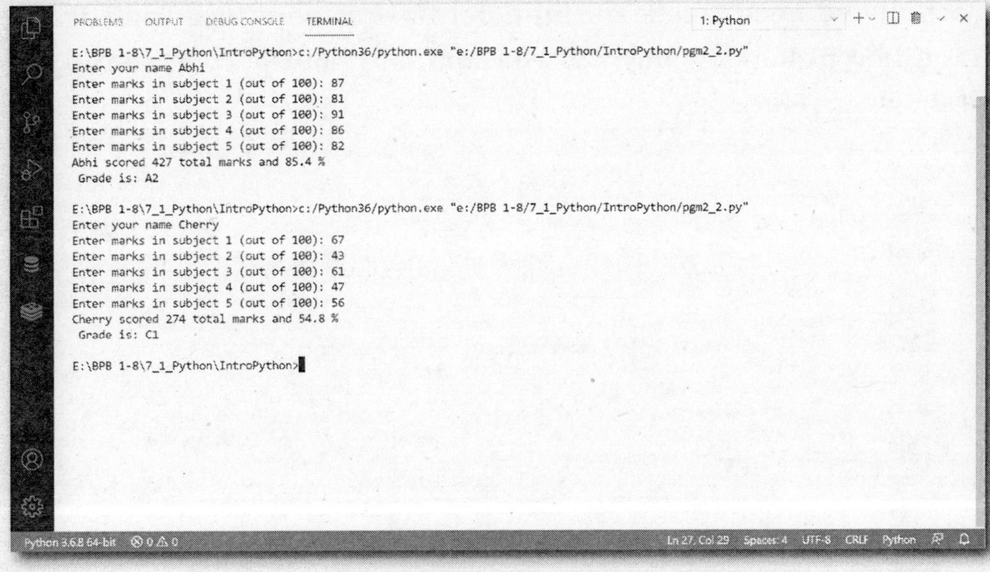
PROBLEMS OUTPUT DEBUG CONSOLE TERMINAL
1: Python
E:\BPB 1-8\7_1_Python\IntroPython>c:/Python36/python.exe "e:/BPB 1-8/7_1_Python/IntroPython/pgm2_2.py"
Enter your name Abhi
Enter marks in subject 1 (out of 100): 87
Enter marks in subject 2 (out of 100): 81
Enter marks in subject 3 (out of 100): 91
Enter marks in subject 4 (out of 100): 86
Enter marks in subject 5 (out of 100): 82
Abhi scored 427 total marks and 85.4 %
Grade is: A2
E:\BPB 1-8\7_1_Python\IntroPython>c:/Python36/python.exe "e:/BPB 1-8/7_1_Python/IntroPython/pgm2_2.py"
Enter your name Cherry
Enter marks in subject 1 (out of 100): 67
Enter marks in subject 2 (out of 100): 43
Enter marks in subject 3 (out of 100): 61
Enter marks in subject 4 (out of 100): 47
Enter marks in subject 5 (out of 100): 56
Cherry scored 274 total marks and 54.8 %
Grade is: C1
E:\BPB 1-8\7_1_Python\IntroPython>
Python 3.6.8 64-bit
Ln 27, Col 29 Spaces: 4 UTF-8 CRLF Python

Figure 2.2 (b): Output window for Activity 2.2

Info bot

while True is a loop that keeps running the code until the break statement is encountered within the loop body. It is used in menu-driven code.

Activity 2.3

A shop is offering a 15% percent discount on Diwali on the purchase of more than 2 items.

Let us follow these steps to solve the above activity:

- Take the input of the Quantity and Rate per unit for all the items.
- Calculate the amount to be paid for each item.
- Calculate the total of all the amounts calculated in the above step.
- Calculate a 15% discount on the total amount if the number of items is more than 2.
- Calculate and display the net amount payable after discount.

In this activity, we need to take the input for the following again and again till the user has different items to buy. So, we require to put the code within the while loop as shown in *figure 2.3*.

```
# Read the quantity and price for each item one by one using loop
while True:
    ctr+=1                 # incrementing the counter for each item
    print(f"Enter the details for item {ctr}")
    qty=int(input("Enter number of pieces: "))
    uprice=float(input("Enter the unit price: "))
    amt=qty*uprice
    totalamt+=amt          # is a shortcut for totalamt = totalamt + amt
    choice=input("Enter quit to exit else press enter key to continue adding
    more items: ")
    if choice=='quit' or choice=='Quit' or choice=='QUIT':
        break
if ctr>2:
    dis=15/100*totalamt

print(f"Total Amount calculated: {totalamt} \nDiscount: {dis} \nBill to pay:
{totalamt-dis}")

```

Figure 2.3 (a): Code window for Activity 2.3

```
BILL
Enter the details for item 1
Enter number of pieces: 2
Enter the unit price: 20
Enter quit to exit else press enter key to continue adding more items:
Enter the details for item 2
Enter number of pieces: 2
Enter the unit price: 120
Enter quit to exit else press enter key to continue adding more items: quit
Total Amount calculated: 280.0
Discount: 0
Bill to pay: 280.0

E:\BPB 1-8\7_1_Python\IntroPython>c:/Python36/python.exe "e:/BPB 1-8/7_1_Python/IntroPython/pgm2_3.py"
BILL
Enter the details for item 1
Enter number of pieces: 4
Enter the unit price: 50
Enter quit to exit else press enter key to continue adding more items:
Enter the details for item 2
Enter number of pieces: 2
Enter the unit price: 20
Enter quit to exit else press enter key to continue adding more items:
Enter the details for item 3
Enter number of pieces: 2
Enter the unit price: 240
Enter quit to exit else press enter key to continue adding more items: quit
Total Amount calculated: 720.0
Discount: 108.0
Bill to pay: 612.0
```

Figure 2.3 (b): Output window for Activity 2.3

float() function returns the number in decimal format from the number or string .

Practice Questions:

- Read a number and display whether it is even or odd.
- Read the year and display whether it is a leap year or not.

A menu-driven program gives options to the user to choose anyone from the given menu. In the following menu-driven program, we will use while loop and simple if-elif-else statements to perform the desired operations.

break statement can be used to exit from the loop body.

Project: Menu-Driven Simple Arithmetic Calculator

Menu-driven arithmetic calculator with the flexibility to add multiple operations.

Code: Menu-Driven – Simple Arithmetic Calculator

```
print("SIMPLE CALCULATOR \nOn two numbers")
while True:
    print("\nMENU")
    print("1. Sum ")
    print("2. Subtraction ")
    print("3. Product ")
    print("4. Division ")
    print("5. Floor division")
```

```
    print("6. Remainder")
    print("7. Power")
    print("8. Exit")
    choice = int(input("\nEnter the Choice: "))

# using if-elif-else statement to choose from the options
    if choice == 1:
        print( "\nADDITION\n")
        num1 = int( input("First Number: "))
        num2 = int( input("Second Number: "))
        print(f"{num1} + {num2} = {num1+num2}")

    elif choice == 2:
        print( "\nSUBTRACTION\n")
        num1 = int( input("First Number: "))
        num2 = int( input("Second Number: "))
        print(f"{num1} - {num2} = {num1-num2}")

    elif choice == 3:
        print( "\nMULTIPLICATION\n")
        num1 = int( input("First Number: "))
        num2 = int( input("Second Number: "))
        print(f"{num1} x {num2} = {num1*num2}")

    elif choice == 4:
        print( "\nDIVISION\n")
        num1 = int( input("First Number: "))
```

```
        num2 = int( input("Second Number: "))
        print(f"{num1} / {num2} = {num1/num2}")

    elif choice == 5:
        print( "\nFLOOR DIVISION\n")
        num1 = int( input("First Number: "))
        num2 = int( input("Second Number: "))
        print(f"{num1} // {num2} = {num1//num2}")

    elif choice == 6:
        print( "\nREMAINDER\n")
        num1 = int( input("First Number: "))
        num2 = int( input("Second Number: "))
        print(f"{num1} % {num2} = {num1%num2}")

    elif choice == 7:
        print( "\nPOWER\n")
        num1 = int( input("First Number: "))
        num2 = int( input("Second Number: "))
        print(f"{num1} to the power {num2} = {num1**num2}")

    elif choice == 8:
        break

    else:
```

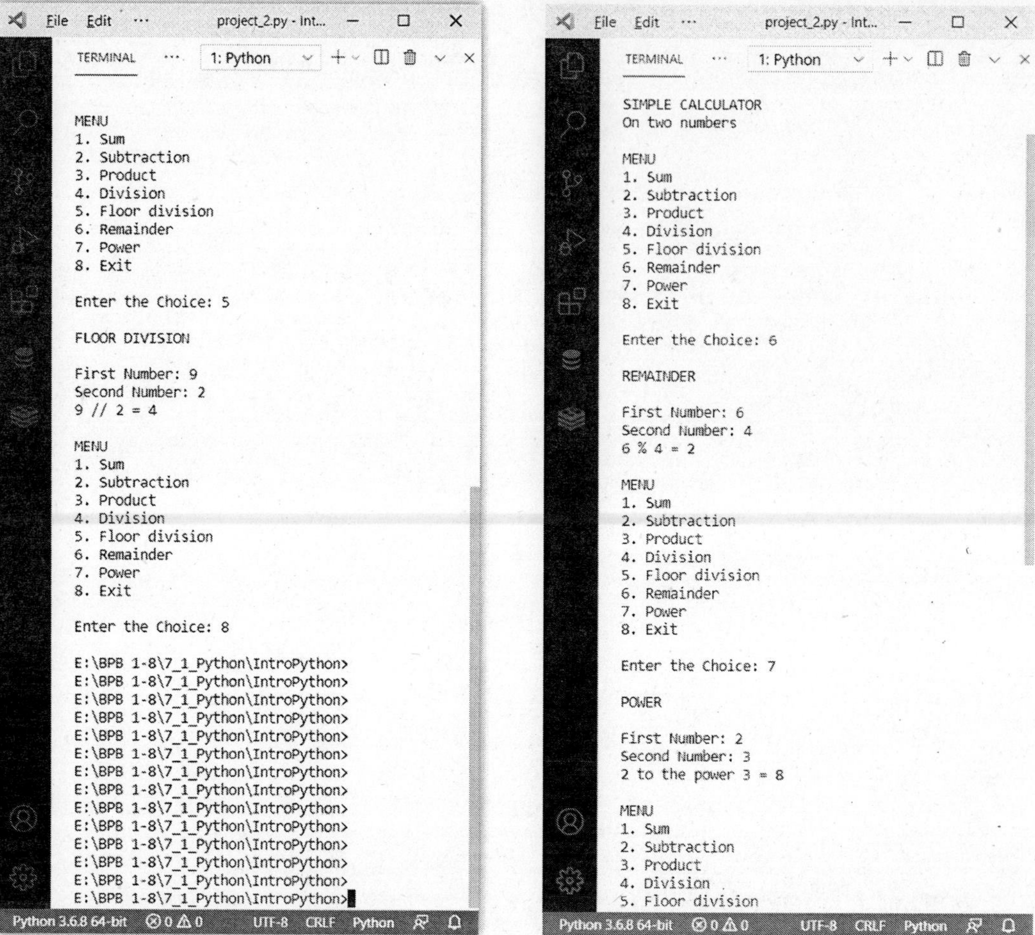

Figure 2.4: Output for the project code

PRACTICE PROJECT:

Create a menu-driven area perimeter calculator for the geometric shapes.

Random Module

Structure

In this chapter, you will learn and practice the following concepts:

- Random module
  - randrange()
  - randint()

Learning Objective

At the end of this chapter, you will be able to:

- build code to generate random numbers within a specific range
- create interesting game
- understand the concept of rolling a dice digitally
- use the concept in the coming chapters to build interesting projects/ games.

PROJECT

Guess the number

Random module

- It is a built-in module.
- Generates numbers randomly.
- Can choose random elements from a list.

We will cover two functions of the random module in this chapter, which are:

- randrange()
- randint()

randrange(a,b): This function is used to return a random integer from the range. It includes the start value but excludes the end value. The step statement is optional.

Activity 3.1

To generate random numbers from 1 to 5.

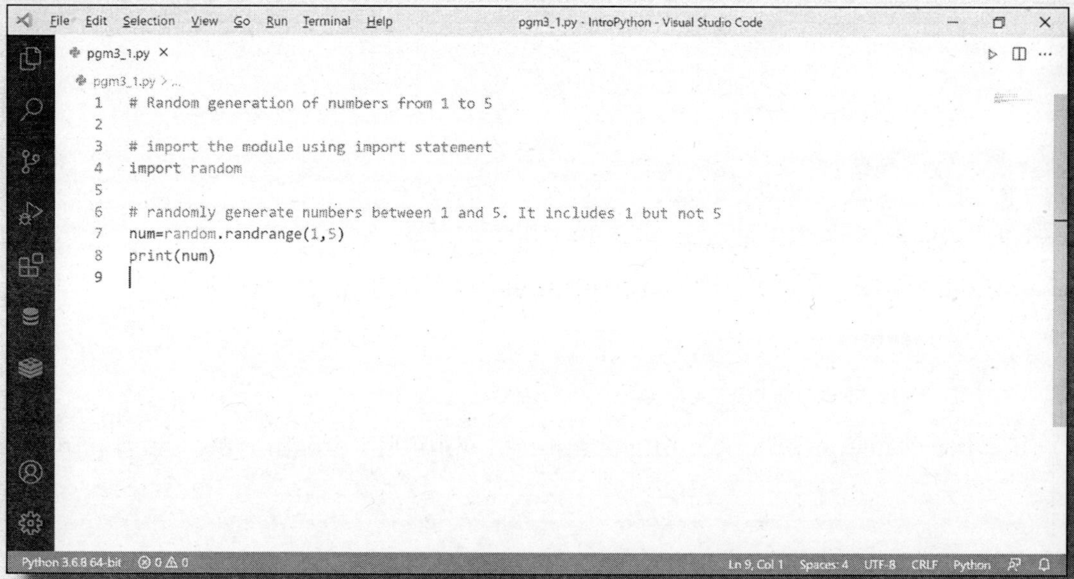

File Edit Selection View Go Run Terminal Help pgm3_1.py - IntroPython - Visual Studio Code

pgm3_1.py

```
# Random generation of numbers from 1 to 5

# import the module using import statement
import random

# randomly generate numbers between 1 and 5. It includes 1 but not 5
num=random.randrange(1,5)
print(num)

```

Python 3.6.8 64-bit ⊗ 0 ⚠ 0 Ln 9, Col 1 Spaces: 4 UTF-8 CRLF Python

Figure 3.1(a): Code window for Activity 3.1

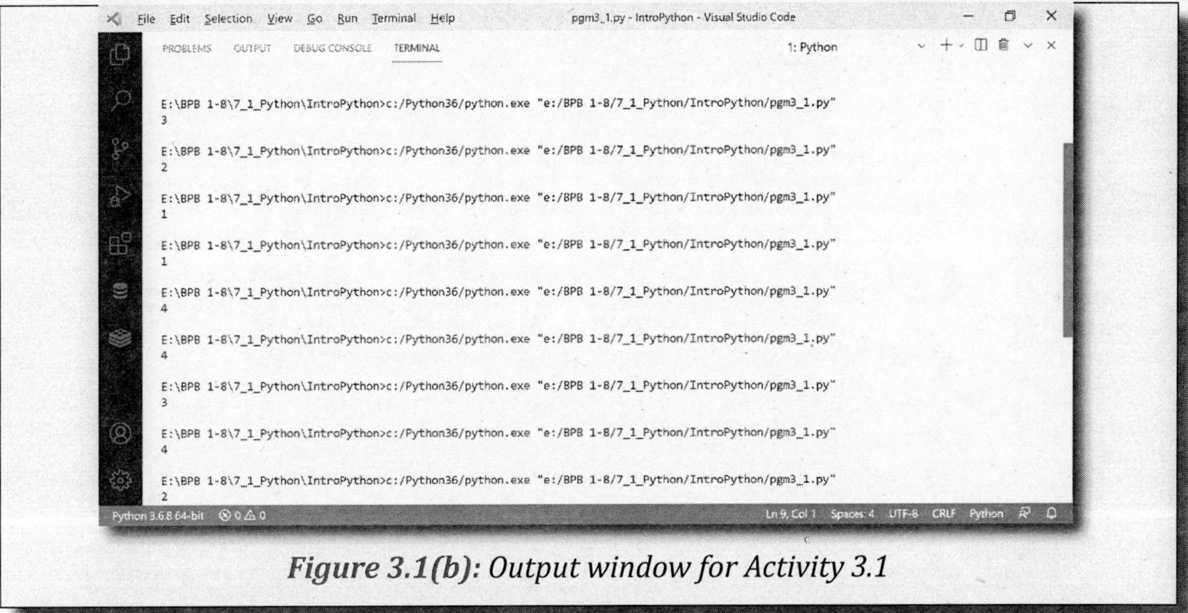

Figure 3.1(b): Output window for Activity 3.1

randint(a, b): This function is used to return a random integer between a and b. It includes both the start and stop values.

Activity 3.2

To generate random numbers between 1 and 5.

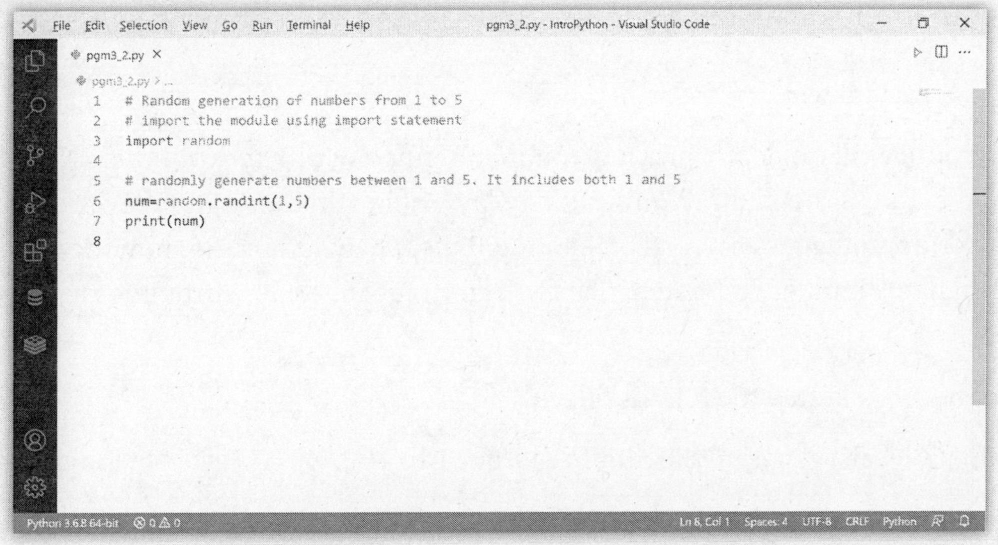

```
# Random generation of numbers from 1 to 5
# import the module using import statement
import random

# randomly generate numbers between 1 and 5. It includes both 1 and 5
num=random.randint(1,5)
print(num)

```

Figure 3.2(a): Code window for Activity 3.2

Activity 3.2

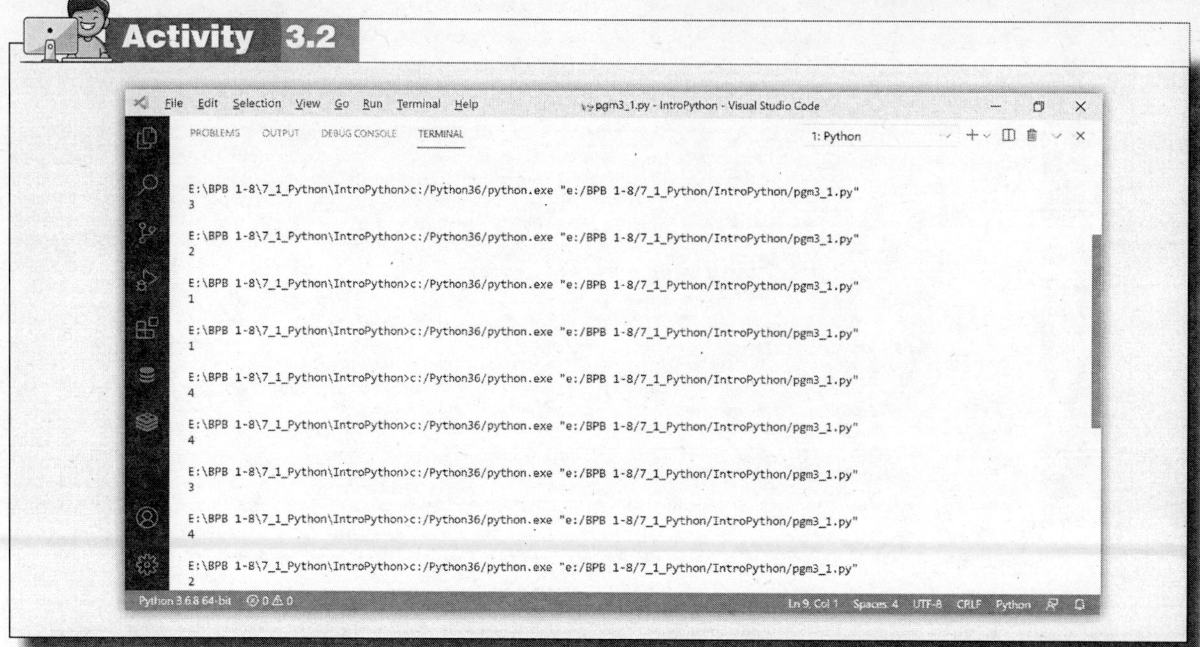

Figure 3.2(b): Output window for Activity 3.2

PROJECT

Guess the number

In this game, the user will be given the option to play:

- Easy level
- Difficult level

The computer will randomly pick any number defined within two numbers. The user will be asked to guess the number. You can display a clue whether a number is even or odd. If the user doesn't guess correctly, then it will display whether the number is greater or lesser than the number generated. This will continue unless the user guesses the correct number.

For easy level, generate the number from 1 to 10.

For difficult levels, generate the numbers from 1 to 100.

Code: Guess the Number

```
# Guess the number
import random

# Game logic begins
while True:
    print("\nGUESS THE NUMBER")
    print("""---------------
            1. EASY LEVEL (1 - 10)
            2. DIFFICULT LEVEL (1 - 100)
            3. EXIT
    """)
    choice=int(input("Enter your choice of action from (1-3): "))

    # Choice Action 1 for easy level
    if choice==1:
        num=random.randint(1,10)
        if num%2 == 0:
            print("Clue: Even number")
        else:
            print("Clue: Odd number")
        guess=int(input("Guess the number: "))
        while True:
            if guess==num:
                print("Congratulations!! you guessed it right. ")
                break
            else:
                if guess>num:
                  print("Sorry! The number is smaller than the guess.
                    Try again. ")
                else:
```

```
            print("Sorry! The number is greater than the guess ")
        guess=int(input("Guess the number: "))

# Choice Action 2 for difficult level
elif choice==2:
    num=random.randint(1,100)
    if num%2 == 0:
        print("Clue 1: Even number")
    else:
        print("Clue 1: Odd number")
    guess=int(input("Guess the number: "))
    while True:
        if guess==num:
            print("Congratulations!! you guessed it right. ")
            break
        else:
            if guess>num:
                print("Sorry! The number is smaller than the guess.
                    Try again. ")
            else:
                print("Sorry! The number is greater than the guess ")
            guess=int(input("Guess the number: "))

# Choice Action 3 to come out of while loop and stops the game
elif choice==3:
    break

# Choice Action if user enters any other number than 1, 2, 3
else:
    print("Wrong choice entered. Please choose any number from 1 to 3 as
    choice of action. Try again")
```

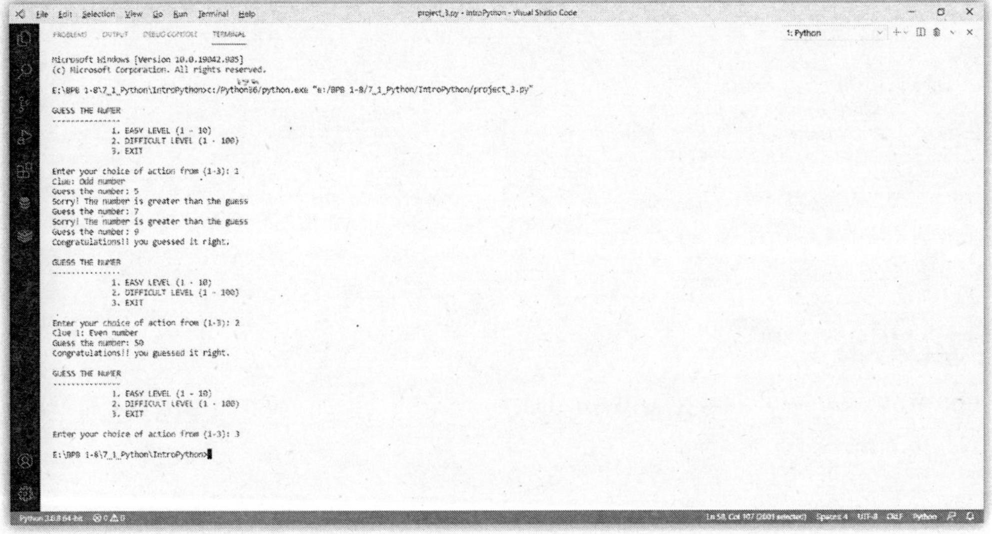

***Figure 3.3:** Output window for Project: Guess the number*

4 String

Structure

In this chapter, you will learn and practice the following concepts:

- Strings
- Accessing strings using positive and negative indexing
- Slicing operator
- Iterating over strings
- Membership operators
- String manipulation operations using built-in methods
  - len()
  - title()
  - lower()
  - upper()
  - find()
  - index()
  - endswith()
  - startswith()
  - isalnum()
  - isupper()
  - islower()
  - replace()
  - split()
- for loop
  - Range function

Learning Objective

At the end of this chapter, you will be able to:

- iterate over a string
- build code using the looping concept
- solve string related problems
- Make use of built-in methods to solve the problems

A string is a sequence of characters enclosed in a single quotation mark or double quotation mark or triple quotation mark. Computers work with numbers and therefore any symbol of the keyboard is interpreted in the form of 0s and 1s internally in the computer to understand. This process of conversion is known as **encoding**. To bring uniformity in encoding, ASCII and Unicode are used.

Each character in a string can be accessed by using the index that starts with 0. The first character can be accessed by index 0, the second by index 1, and so on. Therefore, the index of the last character will be the total number of characters -1.

Python allows negative indexing that means the last character can be accessed by using index -1, the second last character by index -2, and so on.

Encoding is the scheme of character conversion to a number. Decoding is the reverse process of encoding.

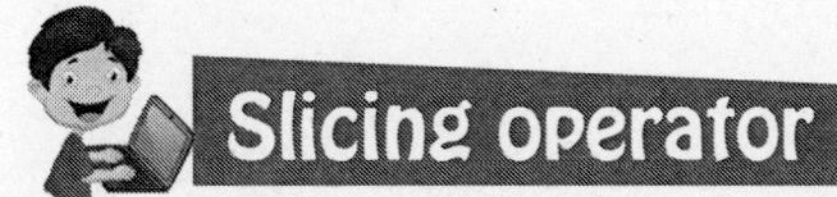

We can also access continuous elements/ characters in a string using a colon (:) symbol known as slicing operator.

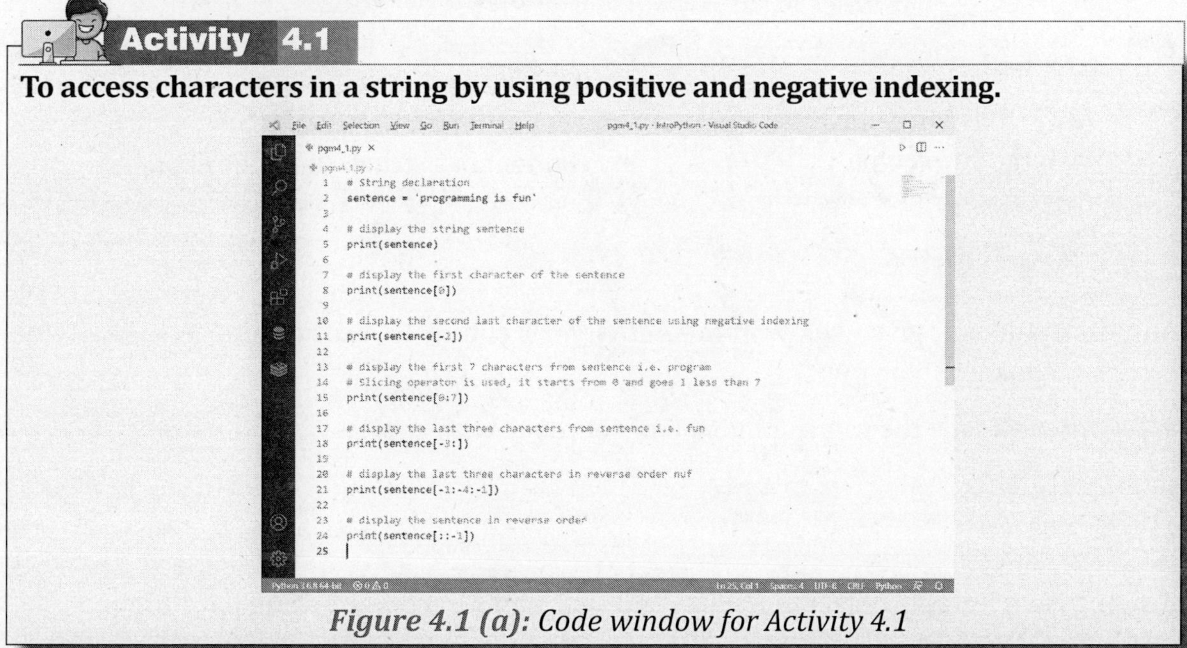


```
# String declaration
sentence = 'programming is fun'

# display the string sentence
print(sentence)

# display the first character of the sentence
print(sentence[0])

# display the second last character of the sentence using negative indexing
print(sentence[-2])

# display the first 7 characters from sentence i.e. program
# Slicing operator is used, it starts from 0 and goes 1 less than 7
print(sentence[0:7])

# display the last three characters from sentence i.e. fun
print(sentence[-3:])

# display the last three characters in reverse order nuf
print(sentence[-1:-4:-1])

# display the sentence in reverse order
print(sentence[::-1])
```

Figure 4.1 (a): Code window for Activity 4.1

Representation of string using positive and negative indexing is shown in table 4.1. The first row of the table shows the string sentence as used in Activity 4.1, the second row shows the positive indexes for the characters and the third row shows the negative indexes for the characters.

P	r	o	g	r	a	m	m	i	n	g		i	s		f	u	n
0	1	2	3	4	5	6	7	8	9	10	11	12	13	14	15	16	17
−18	−17	−16	−15	−14	−13	−12	−11	−10	−9	-8	-7	-6	-5	-4	-3	-2	-1

Table 4.1: Representation of positive & negative indexing

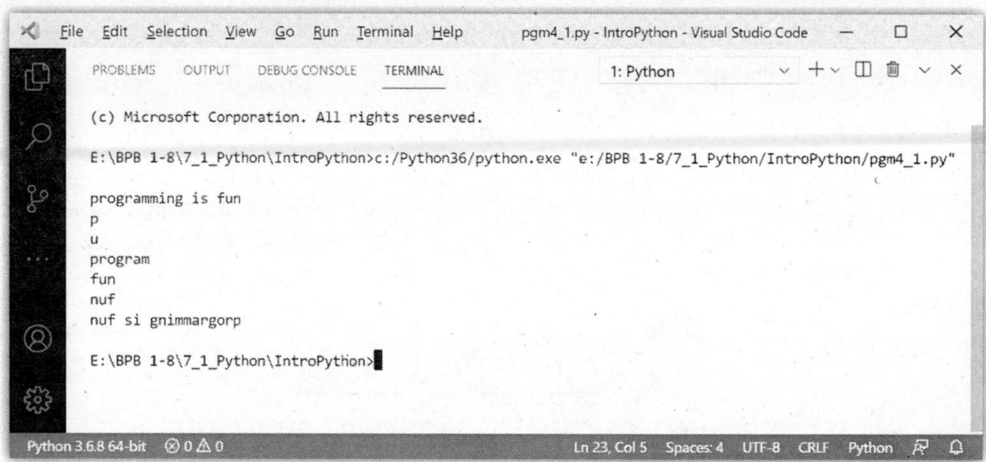

Figure 4.1 (b): Output window for Activity 4.1

input() function returns the value inthe string type.

Strings are immutable by nature which means any element in a string cannot be changed.

Practice Test 4. 1

Add the statement given below in the Activity 4.1 at line 25, execute the code. Write the error in blank given below:

Trying to change the value at index 0 of sentence with capital P

sentence[0]='P'

Error: ______________________________

A string is an iterable object in Python and thus can be accessed using a for loop.

Activity 4.2

Read a string and display the number of times 'i' appeared in the given sentence.

```
# Take input from the user for a string
sentence = input("Enter any sentence: ")

# Create a counter and initialise it to zero
ctr = 0

# Iterating over a string using for loop
for char in sentence:
    if char == 'i' or char=='I':
        ctr = ctr + 1

# Display the number of times i or I appeared in the sentence
print(f"i appeared {ctr} times in {sentence}")
```

Figure 4.2(a): Code window for Activity 4.2

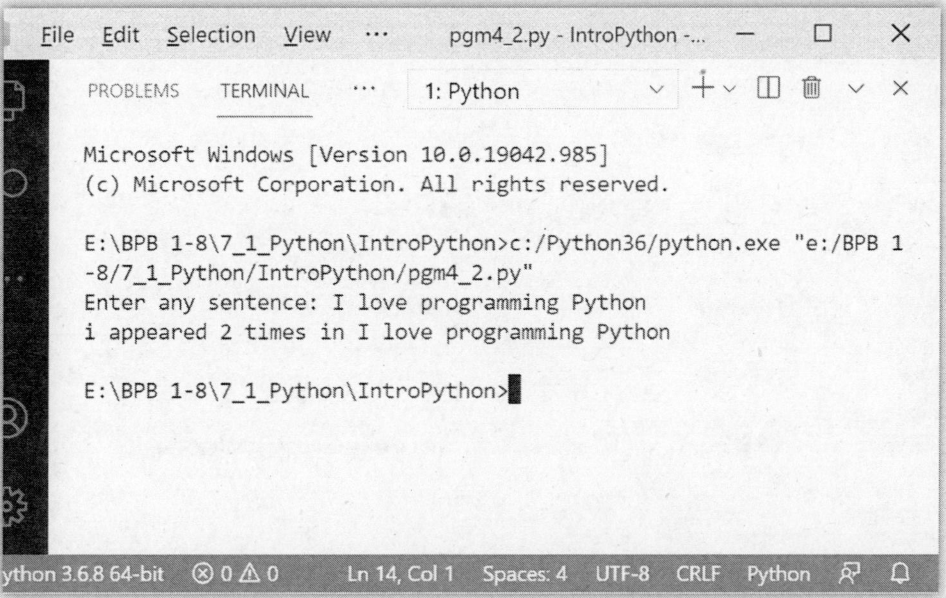

Figure 4.2(b): Output window for Activity 4.2

Use of Logical OR Operator

Logical operators are used in combining more than one conditional statement. Logical OR returns True if any of the conditional statements evaluate to True. As it has been shown in Activity 4.2 while counting the number of times 'I' or 'i' appeared in the sentence.

Info bot

The total number of characters in the string is known as the length of the string.

Activity 4.3

Read a string and count and display the number of characters in it.

```
# Count the number of letters in the string

sentence = input("Enter any sentence: ")

# counter variable to count the number of letters
ctr = 0

# iterating over string
for char in sentence:
    ctr = ctr + 1

# Display the length of the string
print(f"The total number of letters in {sentence} is {ctr}")
```

Figure 4.3(a): Code window for Activity 4.3

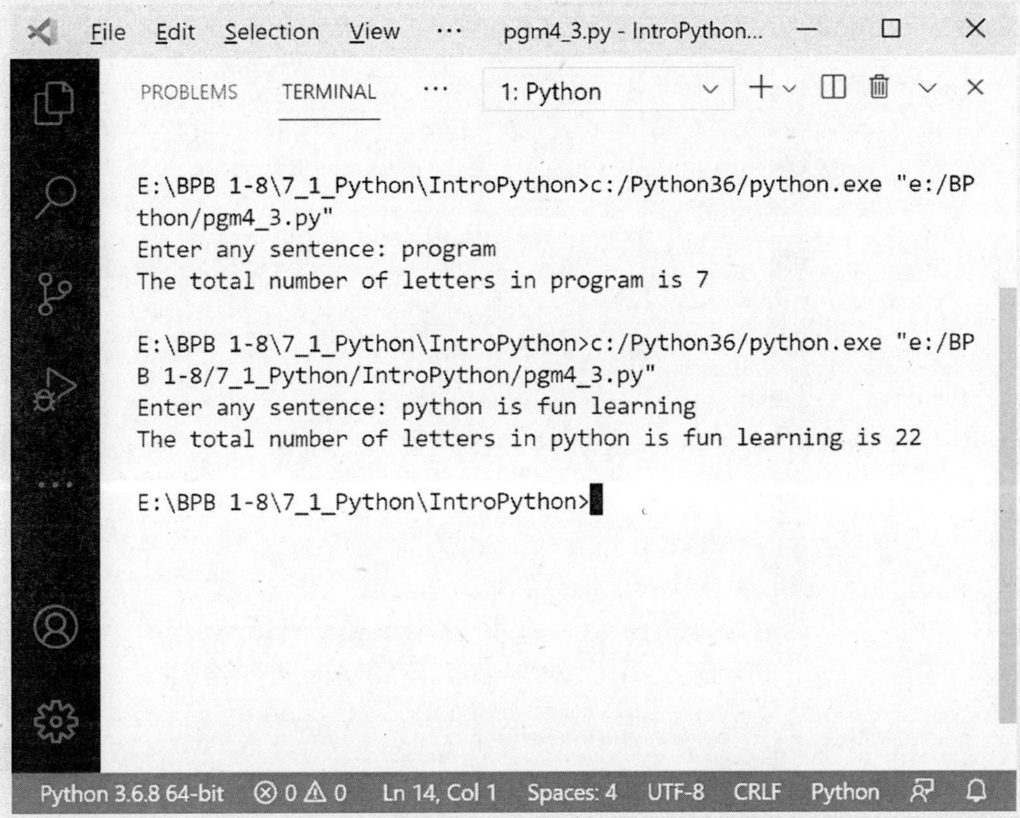

```
E:\BPB 1-8\7_1_Python\IntroPython>c:/Python36/python.exe "e:/BP
thon/pgm4_3.py"
Enter any sentence: program
The total number of letters in program is 7

E:\BPB 1-8\7_1_Python\IntroPython>c:/Python36/python.exe "e:/BP
B 1-8/7_1_Python/IntroPython/pgm4_3.py"
Enter any sentence: python is fun learning
The total number of letters in python is fun learning is 22

E:\BPB 1-8\7_1_Python\IntroPython>
```

File Edit Selection View ··· pgm4_3.py - IntroPython...

PROBLEMS TERMINAL ··· 1: Python

Python 3.6.8 64-bit ⊗ 0 ⚠ 0 Ln 14, Col 1 Spaces: 4 UTF-8 CRLF Python

Figure 4.3(b): Output window for Activity 4.3

Membership Operators

Membership operators can be used to check if the value is present in the sequence or not.

The two membership operators are:

- **in** membership operator returns True if the value exists in the sequence else returns False.
- **notin** membership operator returns True if the value does not exist in the sequence else returns False.

Activity 4.4

Read a string and count and display the number of characters in it.

```
# Calculating no of vowels, digits, words, and symbols
string = input("Enter any string: ")

# counter variables for vowels, digits, words and symbols
vow = 0
dig = 0
words = 1
others = 0

# iterating over string
for letter in string:
    # checking the letter for vowel
    if letter in 'aeiouAEIOU':
        vow += 1
    # checking for the letter for digits
    elif letter in '0123456789':
        dig += 1
    # checking if there is a space then next word is encountered
    elif letter == ' ':
        words += 1
    # if its not a vowel, digit or a space then any other symbol
    else:
        others += 1

print(f"Number of vowels: {vow} \nNumber of digits: {dig}")
print(f"Number of words: {words} \nNumber of other symbols: {others}")
```

Figure 4.4(a): Code window for Activity 4.4

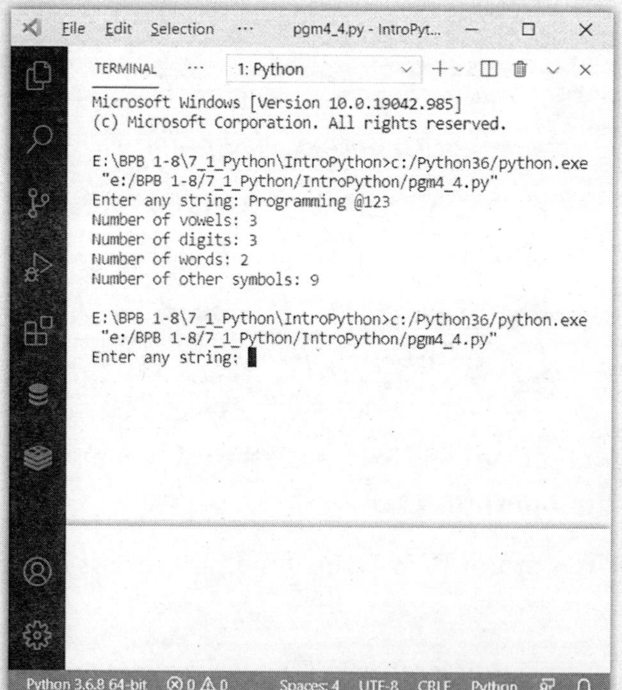

Figure 4.4(b): Output window for Activity 4.4

Activity 4.5

Read a sentence and display it in a toggle case. [Toggle case means uppercase letters to be printed in lowercase and vice versa)

We will be using the following functions in the code to convert letters from lowercase to uppercase and vice versa:

- **ord()** function accepts a character and returns the Unicode of that character. For example, the Unicode for the letter 'A' is 65, 'B' is 66, and so on. Also, the Unicode for the letter 'a' is 97, 'b' is 98, and so on.
- **chr()** function accepts the Unicode and returns the symbol for that. For example, it returns 'C' if Unicode integer 67 is passed to it. It will return a **ValueError** if the integer passed to it is outside the range.

```
# Convert and display the string after toggling
string = input("Enter any string: ")

# new string to store toggled string
new_str = ''
# iterating over string
for letter in string:
    n = ord(letter)
    # checking if its uppercase
    if n>=65 and n<=90:
        # convert it into lowercase
        n = n+32
        # Add the toggled char to new string
        new_str += chr(n)
    # checking if its lowercase
    elif n>=97 and n<=122:
        # convert it into uppercase
        n = n-32
        # Add the toggled char to new string
        new_str += chr(n)
    else:
        # Rest of the letters like space will be added as it is
        new_str += letter

print(f"The new string after toggling the letters is {new_str}")

```

Figure 4.5(a): Code window for Activity 4.5

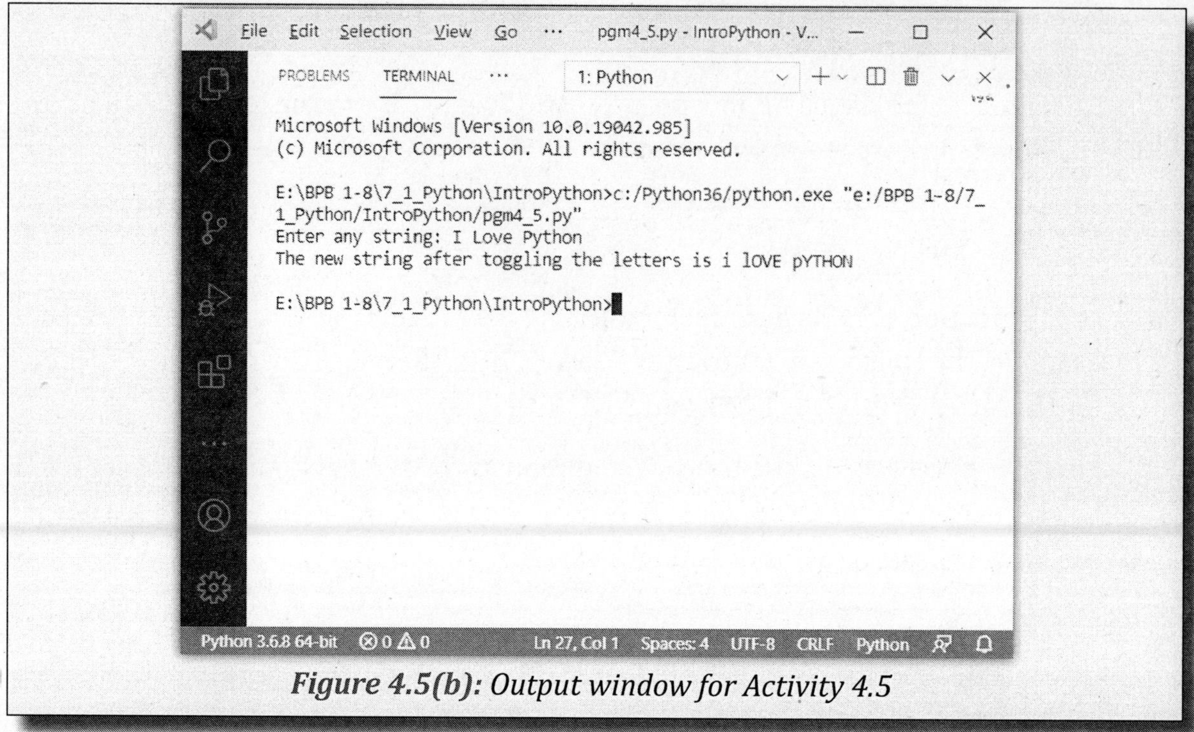

Figure 4.5(b): Output window for Activity 4.5

Try the following to understand the use of built-in string functions in Python

To test these functions in the terminal, click on Terminal at the menu bar and choose New Terminal as shown in figure 4.6(a):

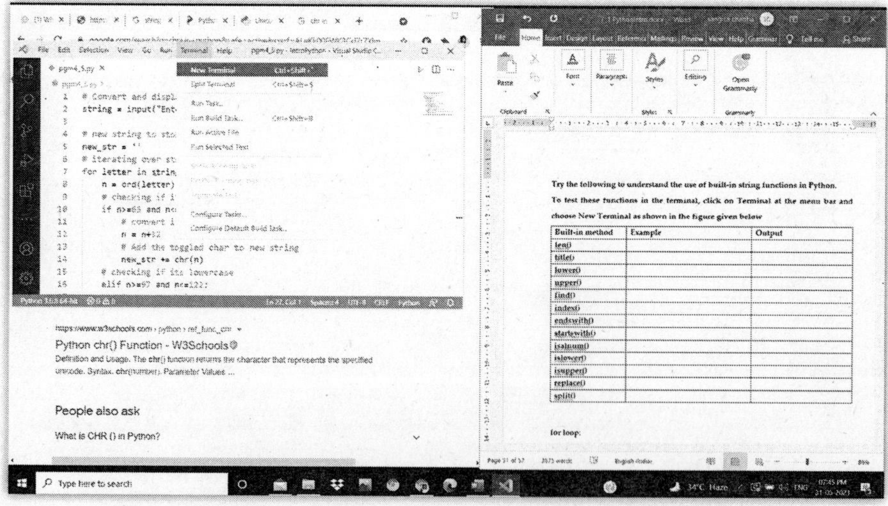

Figure 4.6(a): Step to open a terminal window.

Now type in python as shown in figure 4.6(b) to open Python in interactive mode where you can type in the python statement to test the output.

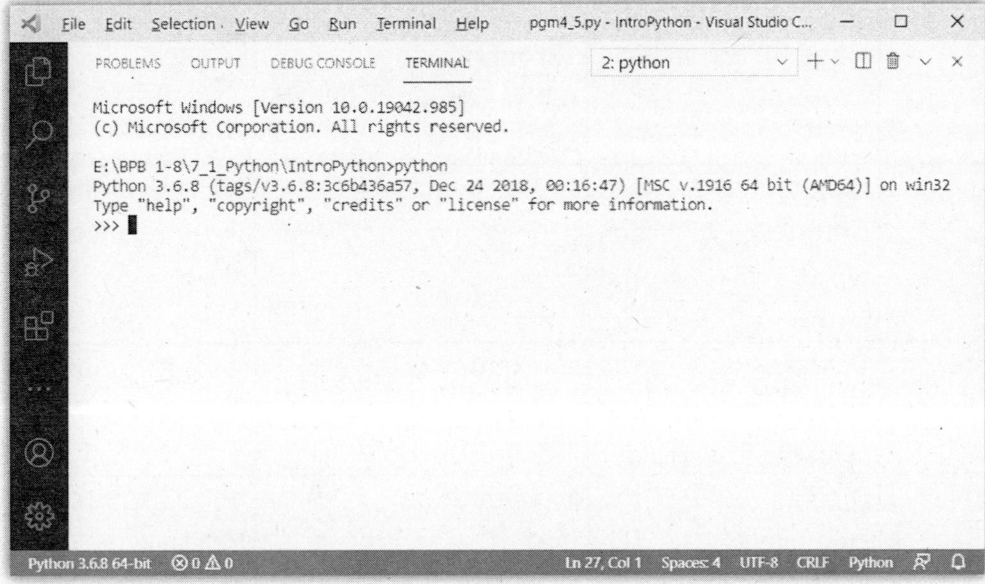

Figure 4.6(b): Open python in interpreter mode to test python statements

Info bot

Interactive mode allows to run the Python statements and gives output immediately after typing in the statement.

Now let us try these in the interactive mode of Python to check and understand the concept and can apply it in the programs.

Built-in method	Description	Example	Output
len()	To calculate the length of the string.	>>> sentence= "Programming with Python is fun" >>>len(sentence)	30
title()	Display the first character of each word in capital letters.	>>>sentence.title()	'Programming With Python Is Fun'
lower()	Display all the characters in the string in lowercase.	>>>sentence.lower()	'programming with python is fun'
upper()	Display all the characters in the string in uppercase.	>>>sentence. upper()	'PROGRAMMING WITH PYTHON IS FUN'
count()	Returns the number of times the substring appears in the string.	>>>sentence.count('i')	3 Returns the number of times the substring appears in the string from starting location till the end location specified. Remember, the end index is not included. >>>sentence. count ('i', 0 , 13) 1
find()	Returns the first index occurrence of the substring.	>>>sentence.find('o')	2

index()	Returns the index of the specified character in the string.	>>>sentence.index('o')	2

islower()	Returns True if all the letters in the string is in lowercase.	>>> str='program'
		>>>str.islower()
		
		>>> sentence
		'Programming with Python is fun'
		>>>sentence.islower()
			True
			
			False

isupper()	Returns True if all the letters in the string is in uppercase.	>>> str1="PYTHON"
		>>> str1.isupper()
		
		>>>str.isupper()
			True
			
			False

split()	It is used to split the sentence/ string into separate words	>>>sentence.split()	['Programming', 'with', 'Python', 'is', 'fun']

Table 4.1: String manipulation functions

for loop: for loop is used for repeating or iterating over a sequence. With the for loop, a set of statements are executed once for each element in a string and list datatype object.

range() function: The *range()* function is used to repeat a set of statements a specified number of times. It returns a sequence of numbers, starting from 0 by default and increments by 1, and stops one number before a specified number. The upper limit is not included.

Activity 4.6

Display the first 10 numbers.

```
# Display numbers from 1 to 10
# start value of i = 0
# end value of i = 9
# step value 1
for i in range(10):
    print(i)
```

Figure 4.7(a): Code window for Activity 4.6

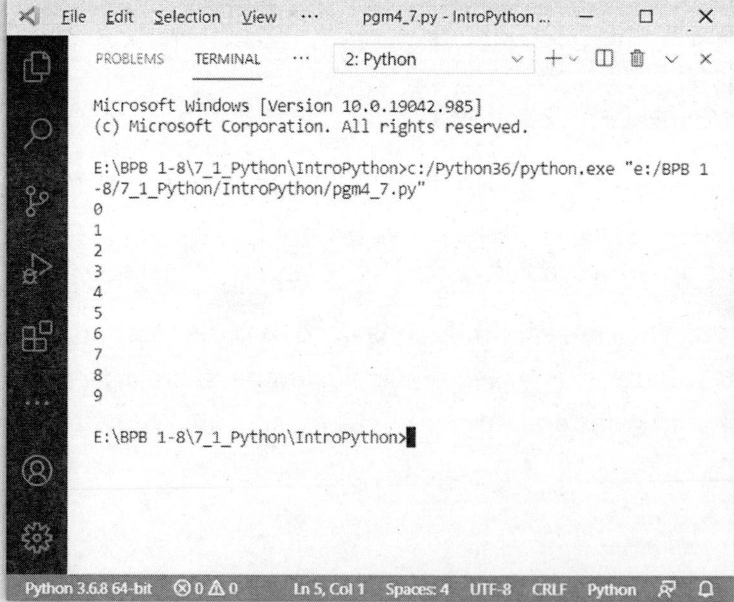

Figure 4.7(b): Output window for Activity 4.6

Activity 4.7

Display odd numbers from 3 to 20.

```
# Display odd numbers from 3 to 20
# start value of a is 3
# end value of a is 20 i.e. one less than 20
# step statement is 2
for a in range(3, 20, 2):
    print(a)
```

Figure 4.8(a): Code window for Activity 4.7

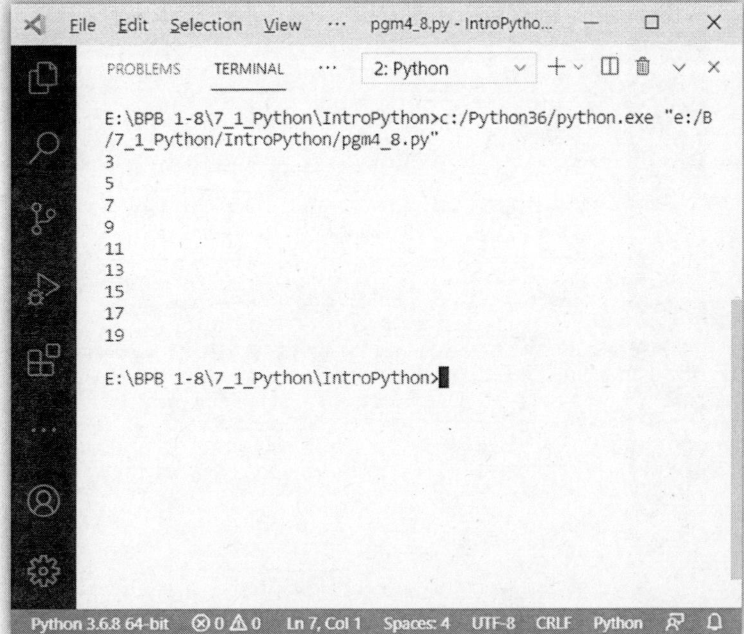

Figure 4.8(b): Output window for Activity 4.7

```
# Display odd numbers from 3 to 20
# start value of a is 3
# end value of a is 20 i.e. one less than 20
# step statement not mentioned so default is 1
for a in range(3, 20):
    # Check if a is odd then display
    if a%2 != 0:
        print(a)
```

Figure 4.8(c): Code window for an alternate way to solve Activity 4.7

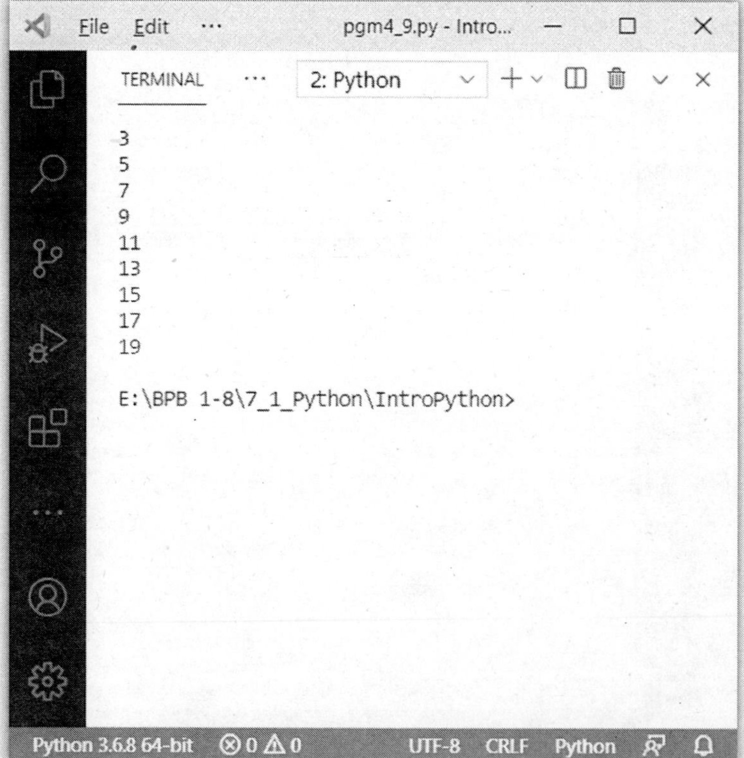

Figure 4.8(d): Output window for an alternate way to solve Activity 4.7

Activity 4.8

Multiplication table

```python
# Multiplication table for a number
# Take input from user for the number
num = int(input("Enter number: "))
# using for loop to start multiplying the number
# by 1, 2 and so on till 10

for a in range(1, 11):
    print(f"{num} x {a} = {num*a}")
```

Figure 4.9(a): Code window for Activity 4.8

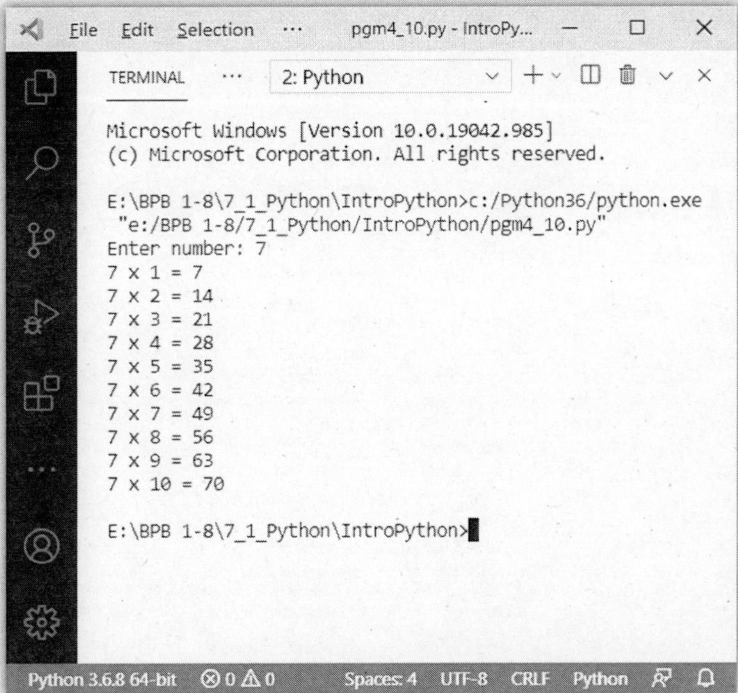

Figure 4.9(b): Output window for Activity 4.8

Practice Questions:

- To read a string, display the first 2 characters and last 2 characters from it
- To read the first name and last name of a person. Display the name using the initial letter from the first name followed by the second name.

  For example, the first name entered is Amitabh and the last name entered is Bachan.

  The output will be A. Bachan.
- Count the number of times a character appears in a string.

  For example, if the string is programming and m is to be counted.

  Then the output will be: m appeared 2 times in programming.
- Print the following series using the range() function

  –2 –4 –6 ... –10
- Sum of first 5 odd numbers

Lists

Structure

In this chapter, you will learn and practice the following concepts:

- Lists
- Accessing elements
- Slicing operator
- Iterating over Lists
- Membership operators
- Built-in methods
- append()
- pop()
- random module
- choice() function

Learning Objective

At the end of this chapter, you will be able to:

- To iterate over a list
- To build code using the looping concept
- To solve list related problems

PROJECT

- Rock-Paper-Scissor
- The Hangman

- A list is an ordered collection of one or more elements of the same or different data types.
- It is mutable by nature which means you can change any element and add more elements to the existing list.
- Store multiple elements together in a list.
- Elements in the list are enclosed in square brackets [ ].
- Each element in the list is separated by a comma.
- Each element in the list can be accessed using the index locations that start with 0 index value. The first element of the list is stored at 0 index location, the second element at 1 index, and so on.
- The list element can also be referenced with negative indexing in the same manner as we did in strings.

Accessing elements

List elements can be accessed in the same manner as we have done in strings.

Let us try these examples using interactive mode in Python:

 # Create a list of numbers

```
>>> numbers = [10, 3, 5, 19, 21]
```

 # print the elements of list numbers

```
>>> print(numbers)
[10, 3, 5, 19, 21]
```

 # Display the second element i.e.3 from the list

```
>>> print(numbers[1])
3
```

 # Display the last element from the list

```
>>> print(numbers[-1])
21
```

Slicing operator

```
# Display alternate elements starting from beginning.

# Here 0 stands for the beginning, a blank after : means go till end,

# 2 after : means leave 1 in between

>>> print(numbers[0::2])

[10, 5, 21]

# Display the list in reverse order.

>>> print(numbers[::-1])

[21, 19, 5, 3, 10]
```

Iterating over Lists

The list is a sequence in Python which is also an iterable object. We can make use of for loop to iterate the list elements. So, you can traverse list elements using the looping construct.

Let us create a list of cities in India.

>>> city = ['Delhi', 'Mumbai', 'Calcutta', 'Madras']

 # Display all the elements of the list city.

>>> print(city)

['Delhi', 'Mumbai', 'Calcutta', 'Madras']

 # Display the city one by one i.e. iterate over each list element using for loop.

```
>>> for a in city:
...     print(a)
...
Delhi
```

Mumbai

Calcutta

Madras

 # Display the city where the first character of the city is M.

```
>>> for a in city:
...     if a[0]=='M':
...         print(a)
...
Mumbai
Madras
```

Membership operators

The two membership operators are in and not in. These operators are used to check if the element matches the sequence or not. The in operator returns True if it matches else returns False.

For example, if the user wishes to display the name of the city which starts with 'M'.

```
>>> for i in city:
...     if i[0] in 'Mm':
...         print(i)
...
Mumbai
Madras
```

Built-in methods

- **append():** Function is used to add a new element at the end of the list.

  For example, let us add a new city 'Chennai' at the end of the list city.

  ```
  >>> print(city)
  ['Delhi', 'Mumbai', 'Calcutta', 'Madras']
  >>>city.append('Chennai')
  ```

```
>>> print(city)
['Delhi', 'Mumbai', 'Calcutta', 'Madras', 'Chennai']
```

- **pop():** It deletes and returns the last element of the list.

  For example, let us delete the last element from the list city i.e. Chennai.

```
>>> print(city)
['Delhi', 'Mumbai', 'Calcutta', 'Madras', 'Chennai']
>>>city.pop()
'Chennai'
>>> print(city)
['Delhi', 'Mumbai', 'Calcutta', 'Madras']
```

Random Module

- **choice():** Function picks a random element from the list.

For example, let us pick a random city name from the list of city. To use the function choice(), we have to import the method random using import statement.

```
>>> import random
>>> print(city)
['Delhi', 'Mumbai', 'Calcutta', 'Madras']
>>> print(random.choice(city))
Delhi
>>> print(random.choice(city))
Calcutta
>>> print(random.choice(city))
Delhi
>>> print(random.choice(city))
Calcutta
>>> print(random.choice(city))
```

```
Calcutta
>>> print(random.choice(city))
Delhi
>>> print(random.choice(city))
Delhi
>>> print(random.choice(city))
Mumbai
```

Activity 5.1

Create a list of numbers, print list, print only even elements, and the sum of even elements.

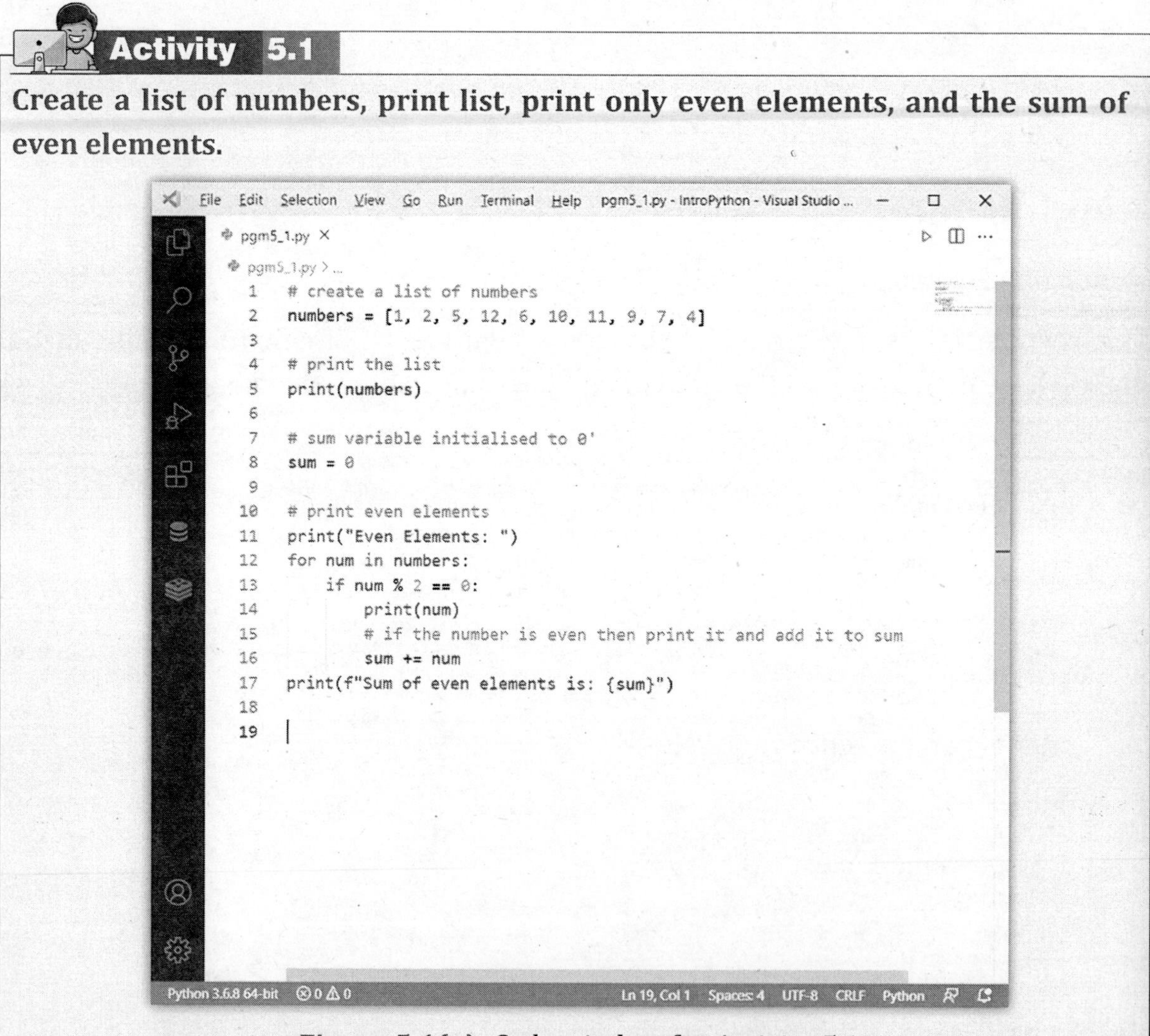

Figure 5.1(a): Code window for Activity 5.1

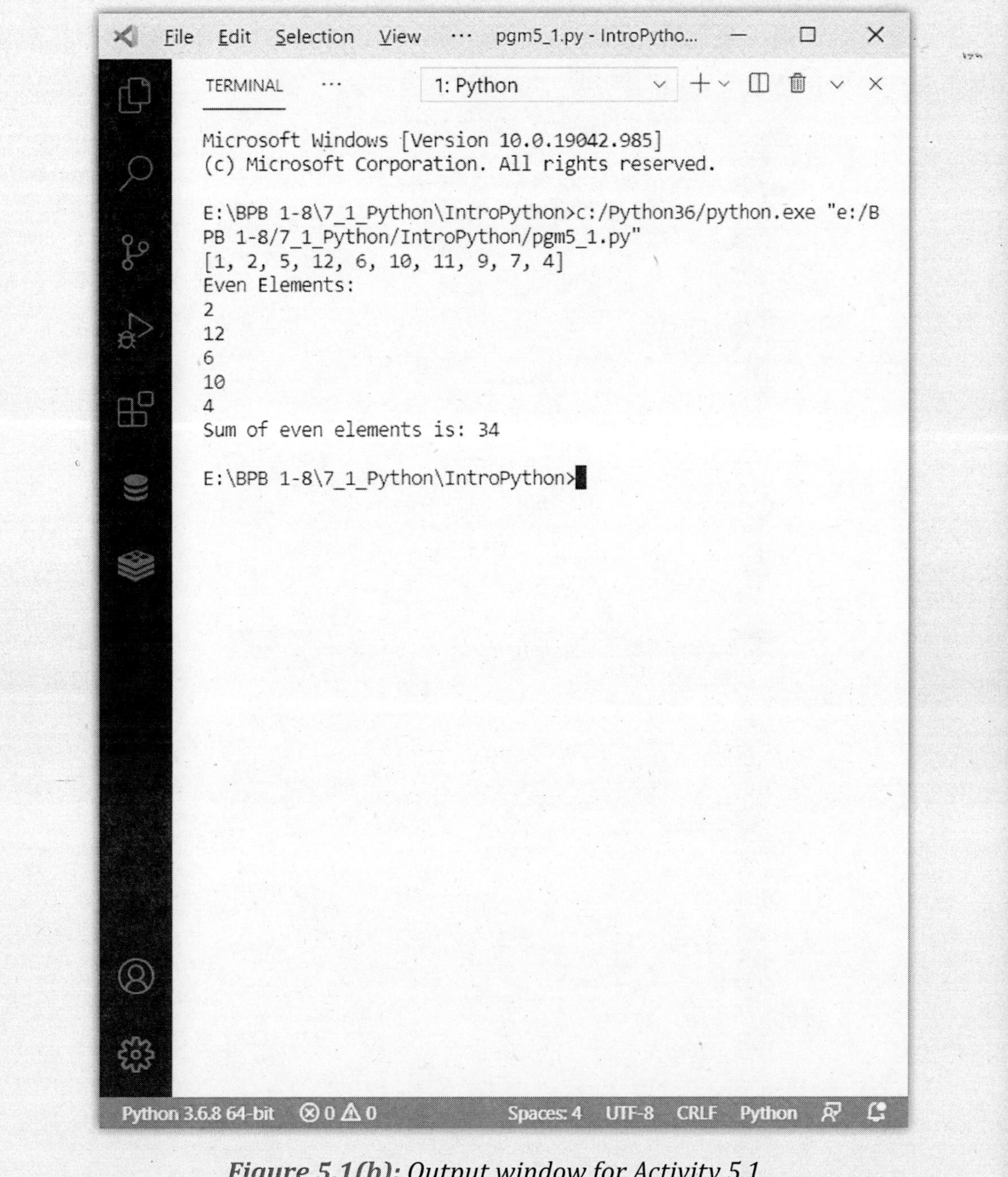

Figure 5.1(b): Output window for Activity 5.1

Activity 5.2

Ask the user to enter the number of elements to be added to the list. Add elements to the list. Display the sum and average of the list.

```python
# Ask user to input the number of element
num = int(input("Enter number of elements: "))

# Declare a list
numbers = []

# Declare a variable sum and initialise it to 0
sum = 0

# Add num elements in the list
for n in range(num):
    # Take input for the number to be added in the list
    x = int(input("Enter the number: "))
    # Add the number to the end of the list
    numbers.append(x)
    # Add elements to the variable sum
    sum += x

# Calculate average as total sum of elements/num
avg = sum/num

print(f"List: {numbers} ")
print(f"Sum of elements: {sum}")
print(f"Average: {avg}")
```

```python
# Ask user to input the number of element
num = int(input("Enter number of elements: "))

# Declare a list
numbers = []

# Declare a variable sum and initialise it to 0
sum = 0

# Add num elements in the list
for n in range(num):
    # Take input for the number to be added in the list
    x = int(input("Enter the number to be added: "))
    # Add the number to the end of the list
    numbers.append(x)
    # Add elements to the variable sum
    sum += x

# Calculate average as total sum of elements/num
avg = sum/num

print(f"List: {numbers} ")
print(f"Sum of elements: {sum}")
print(f"Average: {avg}")
```

Figure 5.2(a): Code window for Activity 5.2

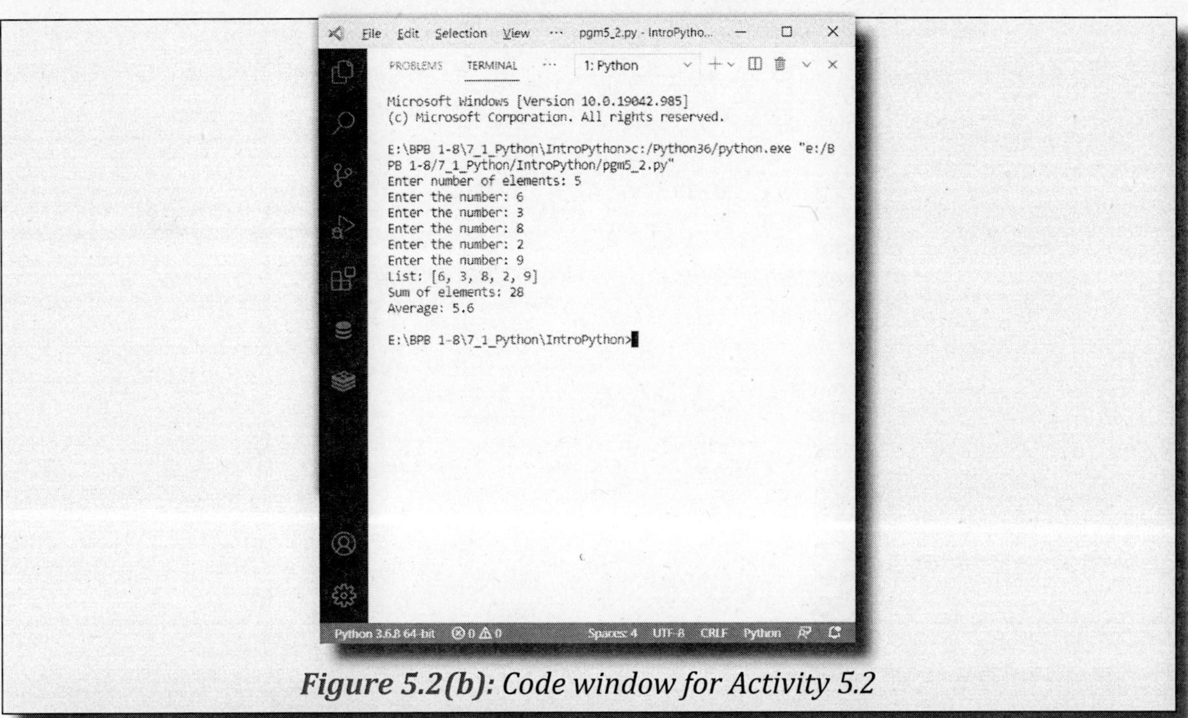

Figure 5.2(b): Code window for Activity 5.2

Activity 5.3

Create a list of colours. Checks and display the position of the colour 'Blue' in the list.

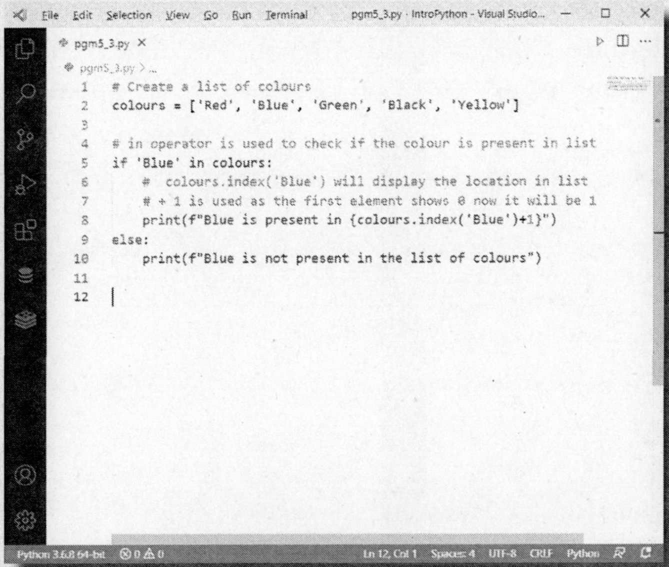

```
# Create a list of colours
colours = ['Red', 'Blue', 'Green', 'Black', 'Yellow']

# in operator is used to check if the colour is present in list
if 'Blue' in colours:
    #  colours.index('Blue') will display the location in list
    # + 1 is used as the first element shows 0 now it will be 1
    print(f"Blue is present in {colours.index('Blue')+1}")
else:
    print(f"Blue is not present in the list of colours")
```

Figure 5.3(a): Code window for Activity 5.3

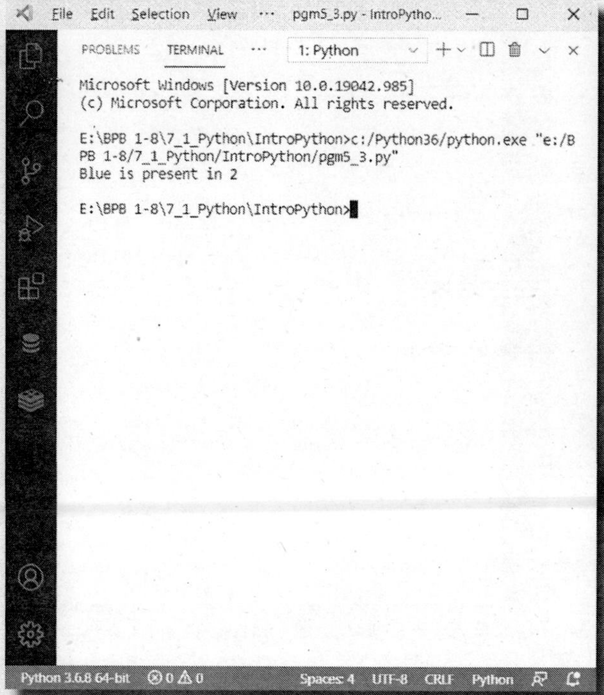

```
Microsoft Windows [Version 10.0.19042.985]
(c) Microsoft Corporation. All rights reserved.

E:\BPB 1-8\7_1_Python\IntroPython>c:/Python36/python.exe "e:/BPB 1-8/7_1_Python/IntroPython/pgm5_3.py"
Blue is present in 2

E:\BPB 1-8\7_1_Python\IntroPython>
```

Figure 5.3(b): Output window for Activity 5.3

Activity 5.4

Create a list of colours. Checks and display the position of the colour 'Blue' in the list.

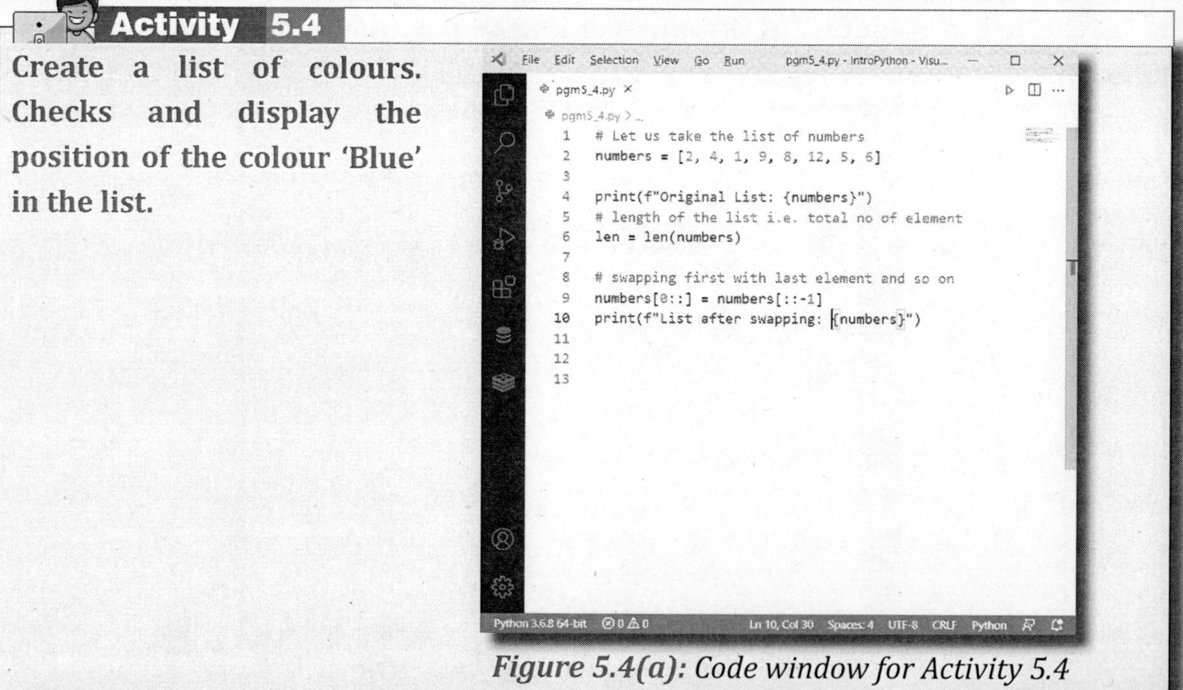

Figure 5.4(a): Code window for Activity 5.4

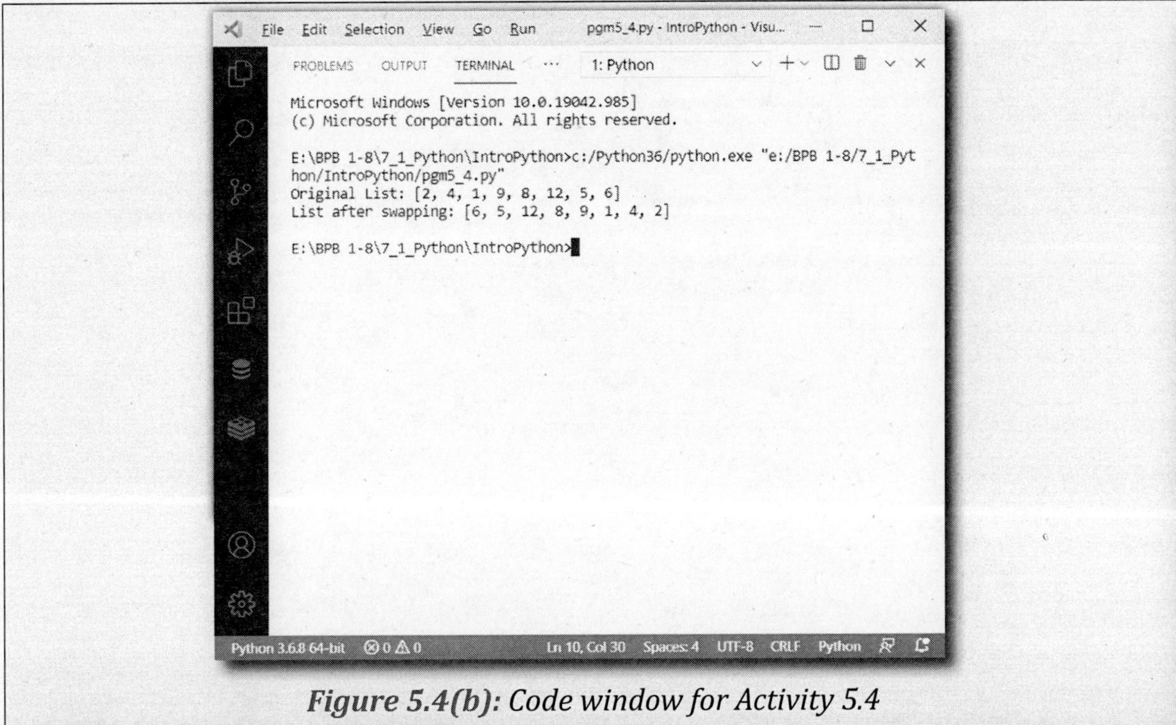

Figure 5.4(b): Code window for Activity 5.4

Activity 5.5

Chennai Super Kings Vs Mumbai Indians

In this activity, the computer randomly picks one cricketer from both the lists of Chennai Super Kings and Mumbai Indians. Display the name of the winner by randomly choosing the winner from both teams.

Display the name of the winning team along with the name of the participant. Also, choose the number of rounds to play the game.

```
import random

# Create a list of two teams
teams = ['Chennai Super Kings', 'Mumbai Indians']

# Create the list of players for each team to add 4 players each
CSK = ['Ruturaj Gaikwad', 'Sam Curran', 'Deepak Chahar', 'Shardul Thakur']
MI = ['Rohit Sharma', 'Suryakumar Yadav','Hardik Pandya', 'Rahul Chahar']

# pick randomly one player from each team to play against
p_CSK = random.choice(CSK)
p_MI = random.choice(MI)

# pick randomly the winning team
w = random.choice(teams)

print(f"{p_CSK} played v/s {p_MI} and {w} is the winning team ")
if w == 'Mumbai Indians':
    print(f"{p_MI} won over {p_CSK}" )
else:
    print(f"{p_CSK} won over {p_MI}")

```

Figure 5.5(a): Code window for Activity 5.5

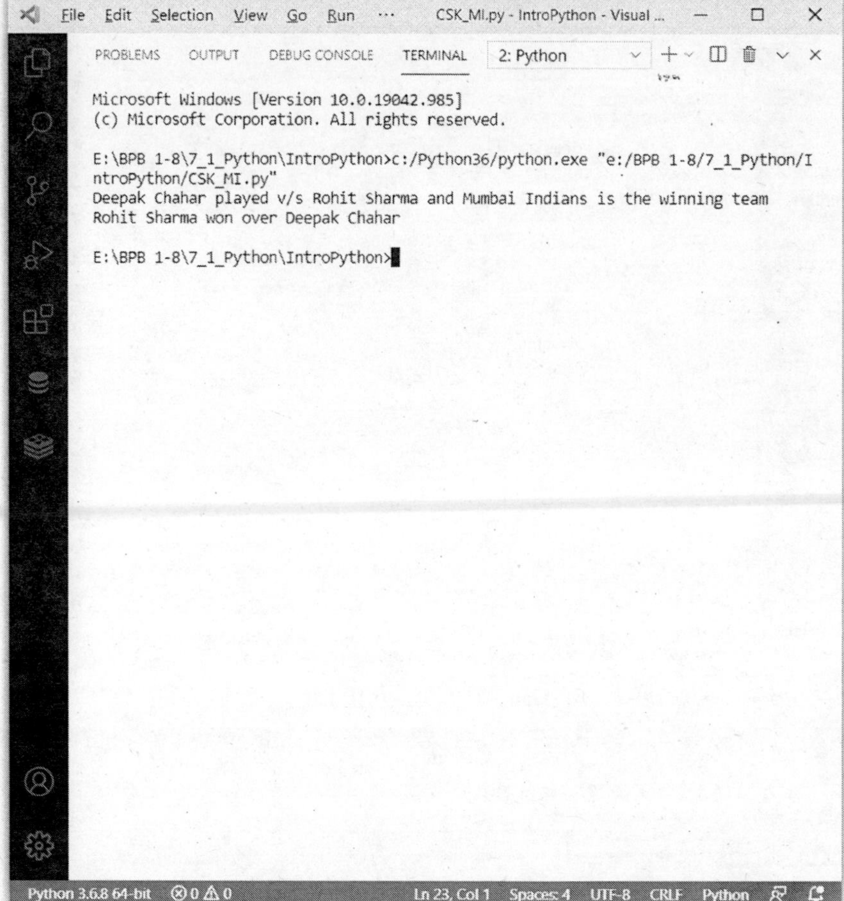

Figure 5.5(b): Output window for Activity 5.5

Project 1

Rock-Paper-Scissor

Build Rock-Paper-Scissor game where the computer is going to pick a random value from Rock-Paper-Scissor and then the user will get a choice to choose a value. Then the winner will be declared using conditioning.

The user will be given an option to play till the user enters quit, point 5 to the winner of each round, and then declare the winner with the total number of points to the Rock-Paper-Scissor game.

```
# Rock Paper Scissors Game

import random

print(" -------------------- ")
print("| Rock Paper Scissors |")
print(" -------------------- ")

options = ["Rock", "Paper", "Scissors"]

pScore = 0
cScore = 0
rounds = 0

name = input(f" Please enter your name: ").upper()

rules = input(f"{name}, do you know how to play rock paper scissors? 'y'
for yes and 'n' for no. ").lower()

if rules == 'n':
     print("Here are the rules for rock paper scissors:")
     print("You have to pick rock, paper, or scissors. The computer will
      also pick one of these three options.")
     print("Rock beats scissors, scissors beats paper, and paper beats rock.")
     print("")
     print("Let us start the game")
     print("")

while True:
     # computer will pick one option using choice() function
     cChoice = random.choice(options)
```

```
pChoice = input("Enter Rock, Paper, or Scissors: ").title()
if cChoice == pChoice:
    print("Tie.")
# Rock crushes Scissor, Scissor cuts paper and Paper covers Rock.
 # Computer is going to be winner
elif (cChoice=="Rock" and pChoice=="Scissors") or (cChoice=="Scissors"
      and pChoice=="Paper")
 or (cChoice=="Paper" and pChoice=="Rock"):
    print("Computer Wins.")
    cScore += 5
# Rock crushes Scissor, Scissor cuts paper and Paper covers Rock.
        # player is going to be winner
elif (pChoice=="Rock" and cChoice=="Scissors") or (pChoice=="Scissors"
      and cChoice=="Paper")
 or (pChoice=="Paper" and cChoice=="Rock"):
    print("You Win.")
    pScore += 5
else:
    print("Choose a valid option to play this game.")

rounds += 1
print("------------------------")
print("")
print(f"Game No: {rounds}")
print("------ Score Board ------")
print(f"{name}: {pScore} | Computer: {cScore}")
print("================================")
print("")

choice = input("Type in quit to exit the game and press enter key
 to continue playing: ").lower()
if choice == 'quit':
    break
```

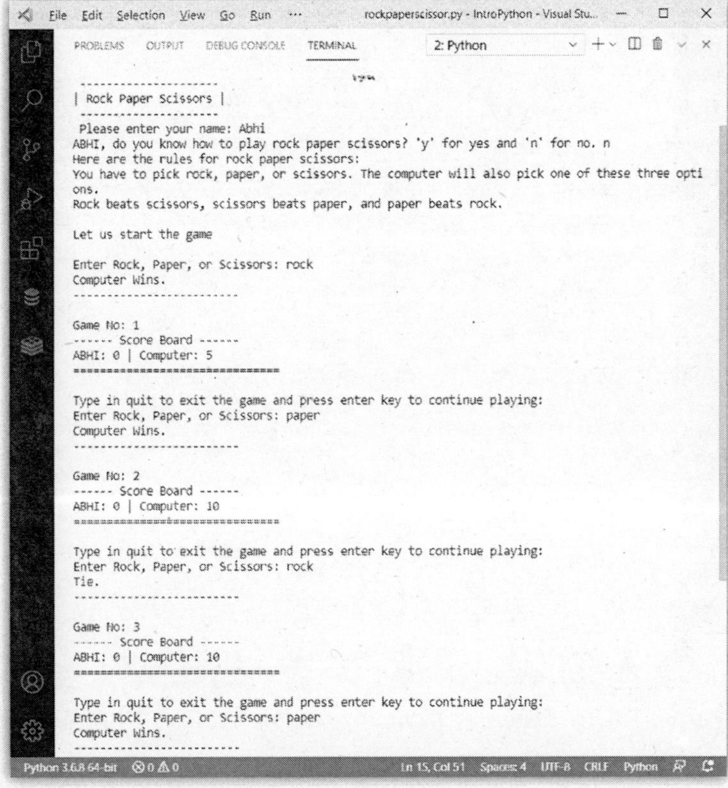

Figure 5.6: Output Window for Project 1: Rock-Paper-Scissors

Project 2

The Hangman

Let us build the PROJECT – The Hangman

To build the project, first of all, let us understand the meaning and the rules for the game.

The word to guess will be displayed by several dashes. The number of dashes will tell the user the length of the word. The computer picks a word from the list of words and then the user needs to guess the word letter by letter. If the letter entered by the user matches with the letter in the word, the code will write it in all the correct positions.

Before we start the code for the Hangman, let us create small projects to understand the concept and then will use that in building the project:

```python
# choosing a word randomly
import random

# check the output by executing it a number of times
# list of month names
mname = ['January', 'February', 'March', 'April', 'May']

month = random.choice(mname)

# now let us display the number of dashes as per the word picked
output=''
for letter in month:
    output += '_'

print(output)

```

Figure 5.7(a): Program Window for Project 2 Part 1 – Hangman

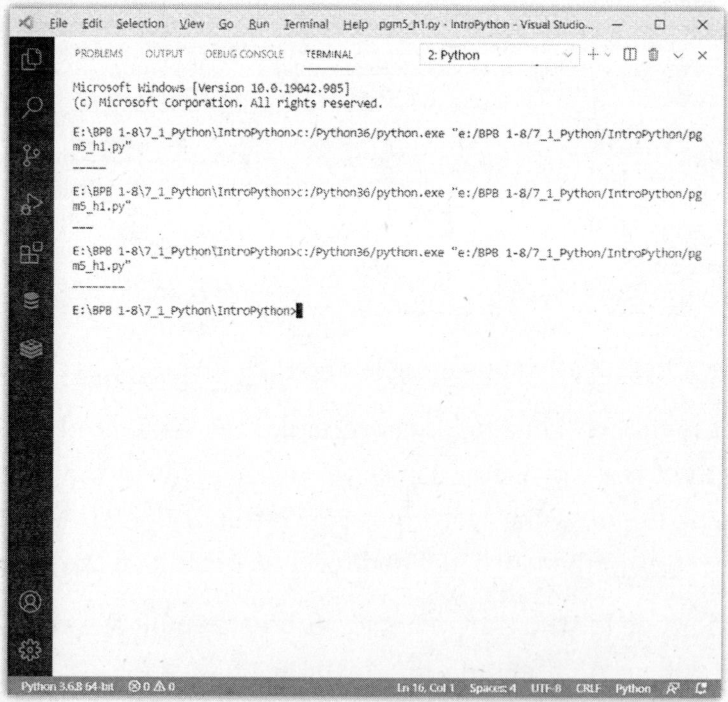

Figure 5.7(b): Output Window for Project 2 Part 1 – Hangman

Let us make changes from line no 10 in the above code to build the game logic as shown in *figure 5.8 (a)*:

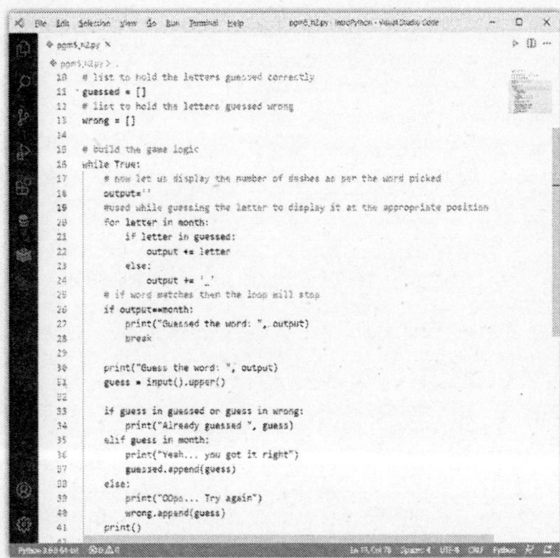

Figure 5.8(a): Program Window for Project 2 Part 2 – Hangman

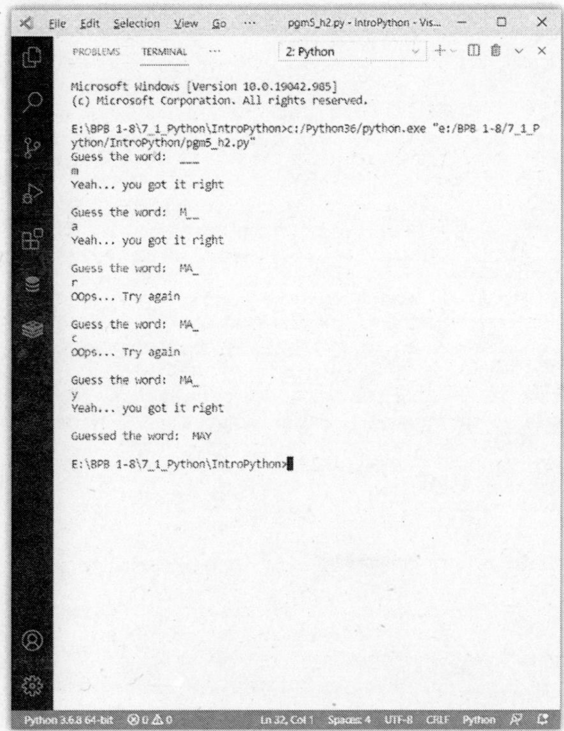

Figure 5.8(b): Output Window for Project 2 Part 2– Hangman

Let us build the hangman using the list and try to use them in the code:

```
# The Hangman
# Let us create the hangman in a list
hangman = [‘‘‘
 +---+
     |
     |
     |
   ===’’’,’’’
 +---+
 o   |
 |   |
     |
   ===’’’,’’’
 +---+
 o   |
/|   |
     |
   ===’’’,’’’
 +---+
 o   |
/|\  |
     |
   ===’’’,’’’
 +---+
 o   |
/|\  |
/    |
   ===’’’,’’’
 +---+
 o   |
/|\  |
/ \  |
   ===’’’
]
```

We have created a list that has a total of seven elements so that it appears one by one when the user guess is wrong. So, the element at index 0 will be displayed when the user guesses the first time wrong, the element at index 1 will be displayed when the user guesses the second time wrong, and so on.

The total number of tries given in the game is going to be 7.

Now, let us change the game logic by adding the number of tries, hangman body to start appearing each time user guess wrong and also add the wrong guess to a list so that if the same wrong guess is encountered by the user again, then it will display an appropriate message.

Also, make use of the list of words having fruits, vegetables, and colours.

```
# FINAL PROJECT
# Will need to add few changes to guess
# choosing a word randomly
import random
# The Hangman
# Let us create the hangman in a list
hangman = ['''
 +---+
     |
     |

   ===''','''
 +---+
     |
     |
     |
   ===''','''
 +---+
 O   |
 |   |
     |
   ===''','''
 +---+
 O   |
/|   |
     |
```

```
  ===''','''
 +---+
 o   |
/|\  |
     |
  ===''','''
 +---+
 o   |
/|\  |
/    |
  ===''','''
 +---+
 o   |
/|\  |
/ \  |
  ==='''
]
# check the output by executing it a number of times
# list of fruits, vegetables and colours
list1 = ['Apple', 'Banana', 'Orange', 'Grapes', 'Pineapple', 'Red', 'Blue', 'Pink',
'Yellow','Purple', 'Onion', 'Tomato', 'Potato', 'Pumpkin', 'Watermelon', 'Muskmelon']

word = random.choice(list1).upper()

# list to hold the letters guessed correctly
guessed = []
# list to hold the letters guessed wrong
wrong = []

# number of tries - keeping to 7 total chances
tries = 7

# changing the game logic here by giving maximum tries 7
while tries > 0:
```

```
    # now let us display the number of dashes as per the word picked
    output=''
    # will be used while guessing the letter to display it at
     the appropriate position
    for letter in word:
        if letter in guessed:
            output += letter
        else:
            output += '_'
    # if word matches then the loop will stop
    if output==word:
        break

    print("Guess the word: ", output)
    print(tries, " chances left")
    guess = input().upper()

    if guess in guessed or guess in wrong:
        print("Already guessed ", guess)
    elif guess in word:
        print("Yeah... you got it right")
        guessed.append(guess)
    else:
        print("OOps... Try again")
        print(hangman[7-tries])#hangman body for word match
        tries -= 1
        wrong.append(guess)
    print()

if tries:
    print("You guessed", word)
else:
    print("You lost and the word is: ", word)
```

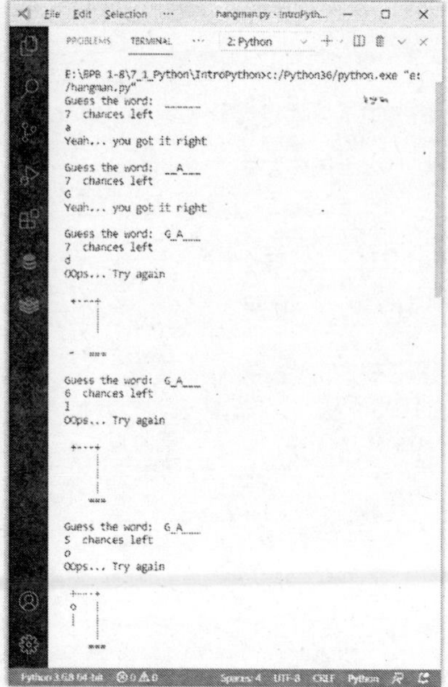

Figure 5.9(a): Output Window for Project 2 Part - Hangman

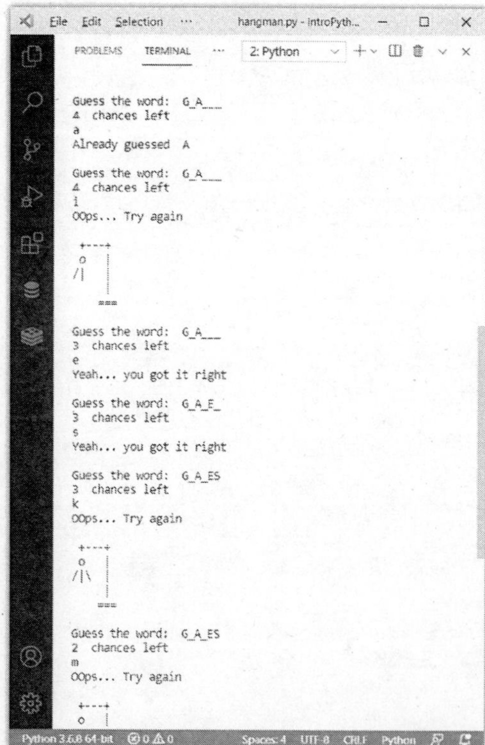

Figure 5.9(b): Output Window for Project 2 Part - Hangman

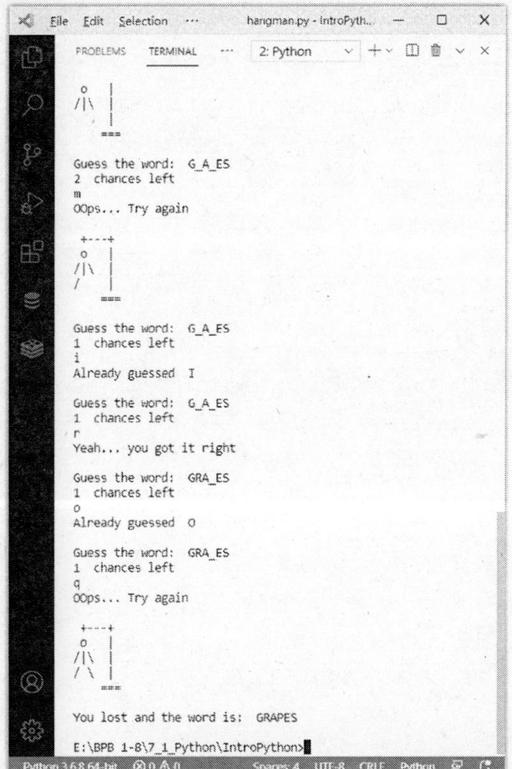

Figure 5.9(c): Output Window for Project 2 Part - Hangman

Practice Questions:

- To print all the odd elements from the list of given numbers.
- To print the smallest and largest element from the list of given numbers.
- To count and print the number of even and odd elements in the list of given numbers.
- To print the elements which are occurring more than once in the list of given numbers.
- To swap the first half of the list elements with the second half of the elements.
- Make use of complete English vocabulary for the Hangman to choose the word from.

6 Dictionary

Structure

In this chapter, you will learn and practice the following concepts:

- Dictionary
- Accessing elements
- Iterating over Dictionary
- Dictionary functions
  - get()
  - key()
  - values()
  - items()

Learning Objective

At the end of this chapter, you will be able to:

- To store data in the form of key: value pairs
- To display the value for any key or associated key for the given value
- To solve dictionary related problems

PROJECT

Interactive Dictionary

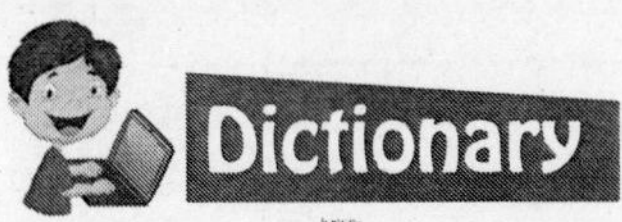

- Each item in a dictionary has a key and a corresponding value i.e. (key: value pair).
- The key and value are separated with a colon (:).
- It is declared within curly parenthesis {}.
- Different elements are separated by a comma (,).
- Values can be of any data type and can repeat.
- Keys must be of immutable type (string, number, or tuple) and must be unique.

Accessing elements

- Dictionary uses keys to access the values.
- Keys can be used either with square brackets [ ] or with the get() method.

Activity 6.1

Create a dictionary of fruits to store the fruit name and price as key: value pair. Add a new fruit to the dictionary. Display the dictionary, fruit name, and the respective price.

```
# Create a dictionary fruits to store fruit name and its price
fruits = {'Apple': 120, 'Banana': 60, 'Mango': 80, 'Pineapple': 150, 'Cherry': 200}

# Display the dictionary
print(f"The dictionary is: {fruits}")

# Display each element of dictionary one by one
print("Keys in the dictionary: ")
for i in fruits:
    # i represent the key in fruits and
    # fruits[i] will give its respective value
    print(f"{i} has price {fruits[i]}")

# Displaying only the keys using key() function
print(f"Keys in the dictionary are: {fruits.keys()}")

# Displaying only the values using values() function
print(f"Values in the dictionary are: {fruits.values()}")

# Adding a new fruit in the dictionary
fruits['Kiwi'] = 300

# Display the dictionary
print(f"Dictionary : {fruits}")

```

Figure 6.1(a): Code window for Activity 6.1

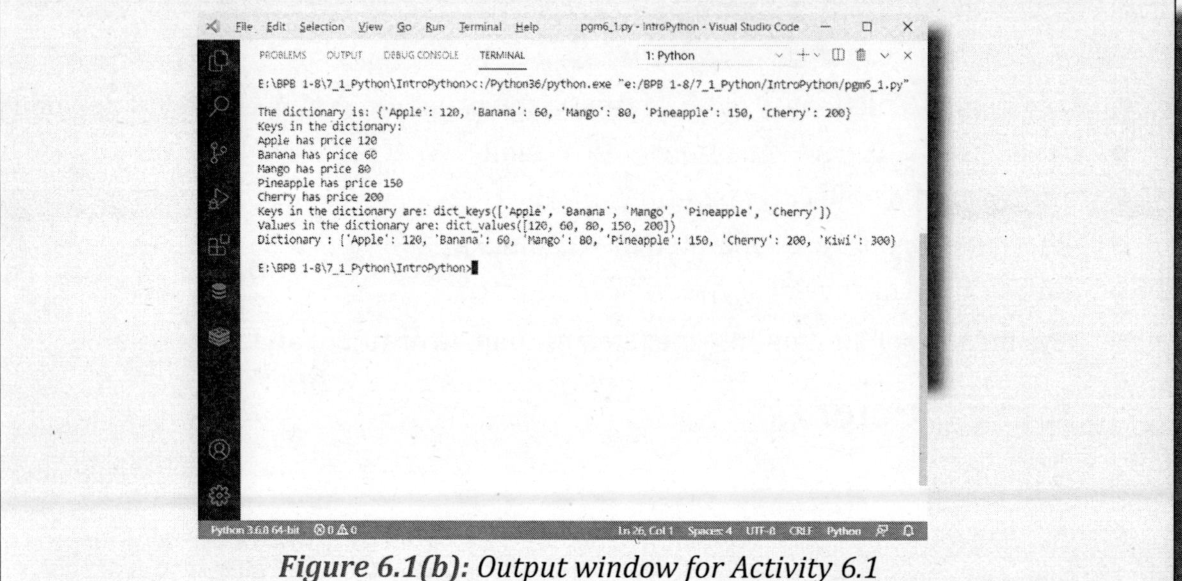

Figure 6.1(b): Output window for Activity 6.1

Activity 6.2

Create a dictionary that has each item a pair of a number and its cube from numbers 1 to 5.

In this activity, we have to take the numbers from 1 to 5 as key and the corresponding value needs to be calculated as the cube of the key.

```
# create empty dictionary
cube_dict = {}

# keys in the dictionary are the numbers from 1 to 5
# value is the cube of the corresponding key
# for loop will assign values 1 to 5 to key
for key in range(1, 6):
    # key will have cube of key as value
    cube_dict[key] = key**3

print(f"Cube dictionary: {cube_dict}")
```

Figure 6.2(a): Code window for Activity 6.2

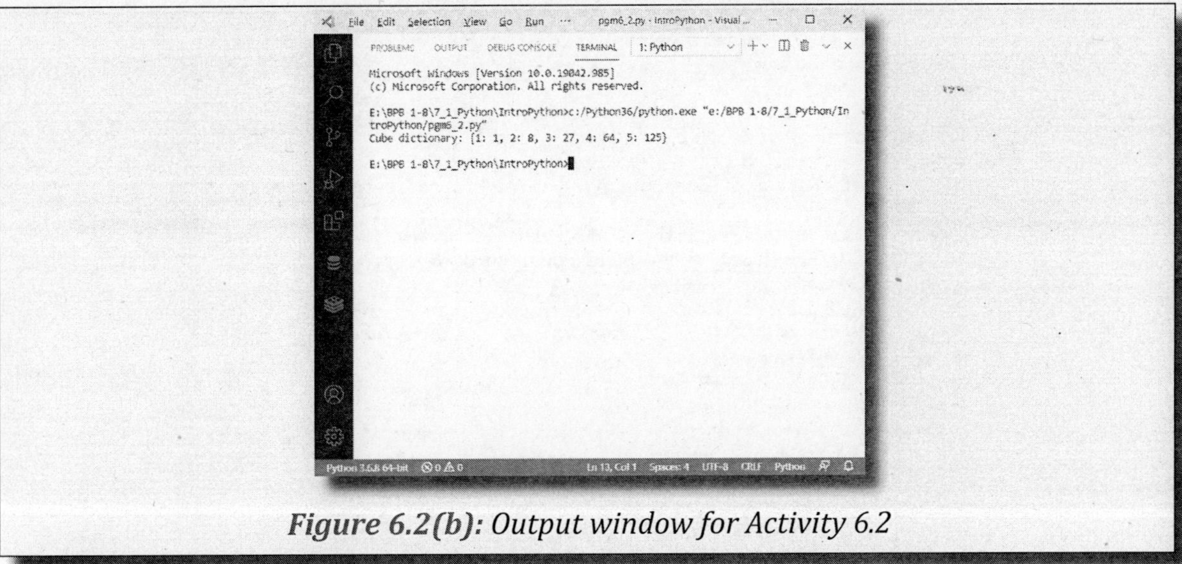

Figure 6.2(b): Output window for Activity 6.2

Activity 6.3

Create a dictionary to store the month names as keys and the number of days as the values for the respective months. Print the dictionary, only the month names, the days in the month, and then months with the number of days as 31.

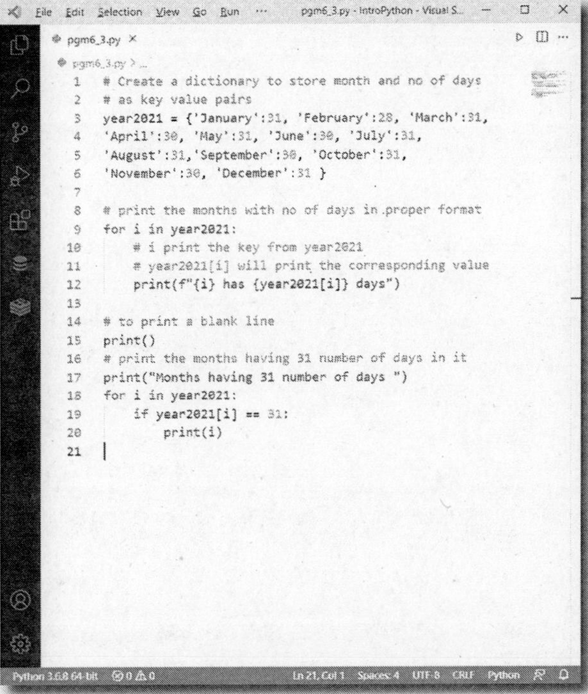

Figure 6.3(a): Code window for Activity 6.3

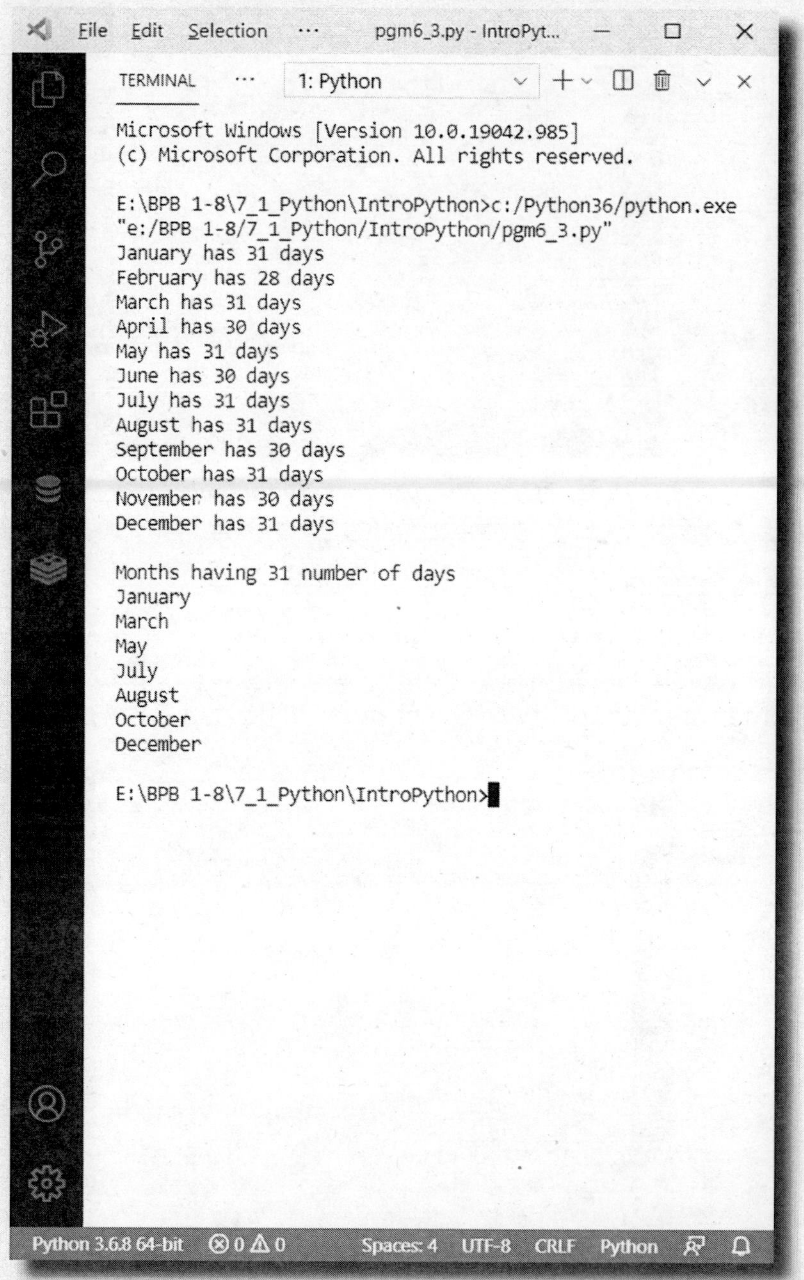

Figure 6.3(b): Output window for Activity 6.3

Activity 6.4

Find out the frequency of characters appearing in the word user inputs.

```
# Read a string
string = input("Enter any string: ")

# Declare a dictionary to create character as key
# frequency of that character in the string is its value
freq = {}

# string is an iterable object
# iterate over string using for loop
for letter in string:
    # check if the letter already exists in the dictionary
    # if it exists then the value will be incremented by 1
    if letter in freq:
        freq[letter] += 1
    else:
        # if letter is not there in dictionary
        # it creates it as as key and assign value 1 to it
        freq[letter] = 1

# Display the string
print(f"Entered string is {string}")
# Display the dictionary
print(f"Frequency of characters: {freq}")
```

Figure 6.4(a): Code window for Activity 6.4

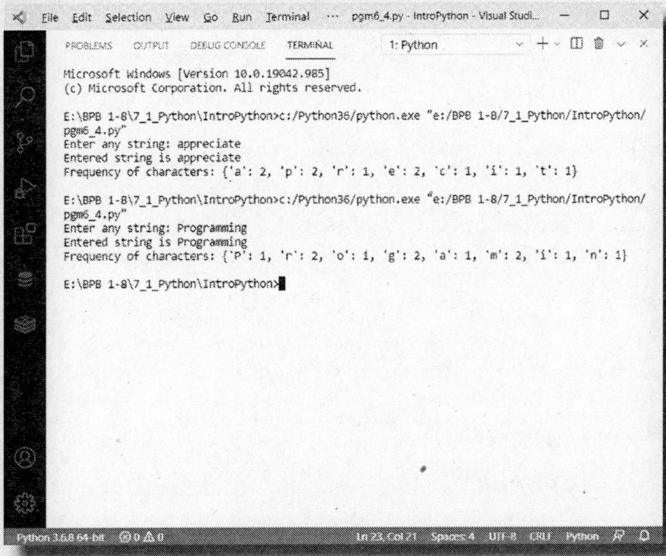

Figure 6.4(b): Output window for Activity 6.4

Project

Interactive Dictionary

- Interactive Dictionary is a menu-driven project in which you have the following options for the user:
- Add a new word and meaning to the interactive dictionary.
- Want to search for the meaning of any word from the dictionary.
- Exit.

```
# Menu-driven Interactive Dictionary
# declared a dictionary with few words as key and
# meanings as value

word_meanings = {
'appreciate':'recognize the full worth of',
'ratitude':'the quality of being thankful',
'apple':'red or green color, round fruit',
'orange':'reddish-yellow, a large round juicy citrus fruit',
'kiwi':'fruit with a thin hairy skin, green flesh, & black seeds',
'watermelon':'large fruit with a hard green striped,sweet watery pink',
'mango':'large oblong fruit with a firm yellowish-red skin',
'lemon':'an acid fruit'
}

# Project Logic
while True:
    print("""
    =========================
    INTERACTIVE DICTIONARY
    =========================
    """)
```

```
# Options to choose from
print("1. Add new word meaning")
print("2. Search" for word meaning")
print("3. Exit")
# Take the value from user as choice of action
choice = int(input("Enter your choice (1-3): "))
if choice == 1:
    # Take the new word
    word = input("Enter new word: ").lower()
    # Provide meaning for that word
    meaning = input("Enter meaning: ").lower()
    if word in word_meanings:
        print("Sorry!! word already exists. Try again!")
    else:
        word_meanings[word] = meaning
elif choice == 2:
    word = input("Enter word to look for the meaning: ").lower()
    # check if word exists in the key of the dictionary
    if word in word_meanings:
        # display the word and its meaning from the dictionary
        print(f"{word} means {word_meanings[word]}")
    else:
     #otherwise display message that word is not in dictionary
        print(f"Sorry! {word} is not in my dictionary! ")
elif choice == 3:
    break
else:
    print("Wrong choice entered ")
```

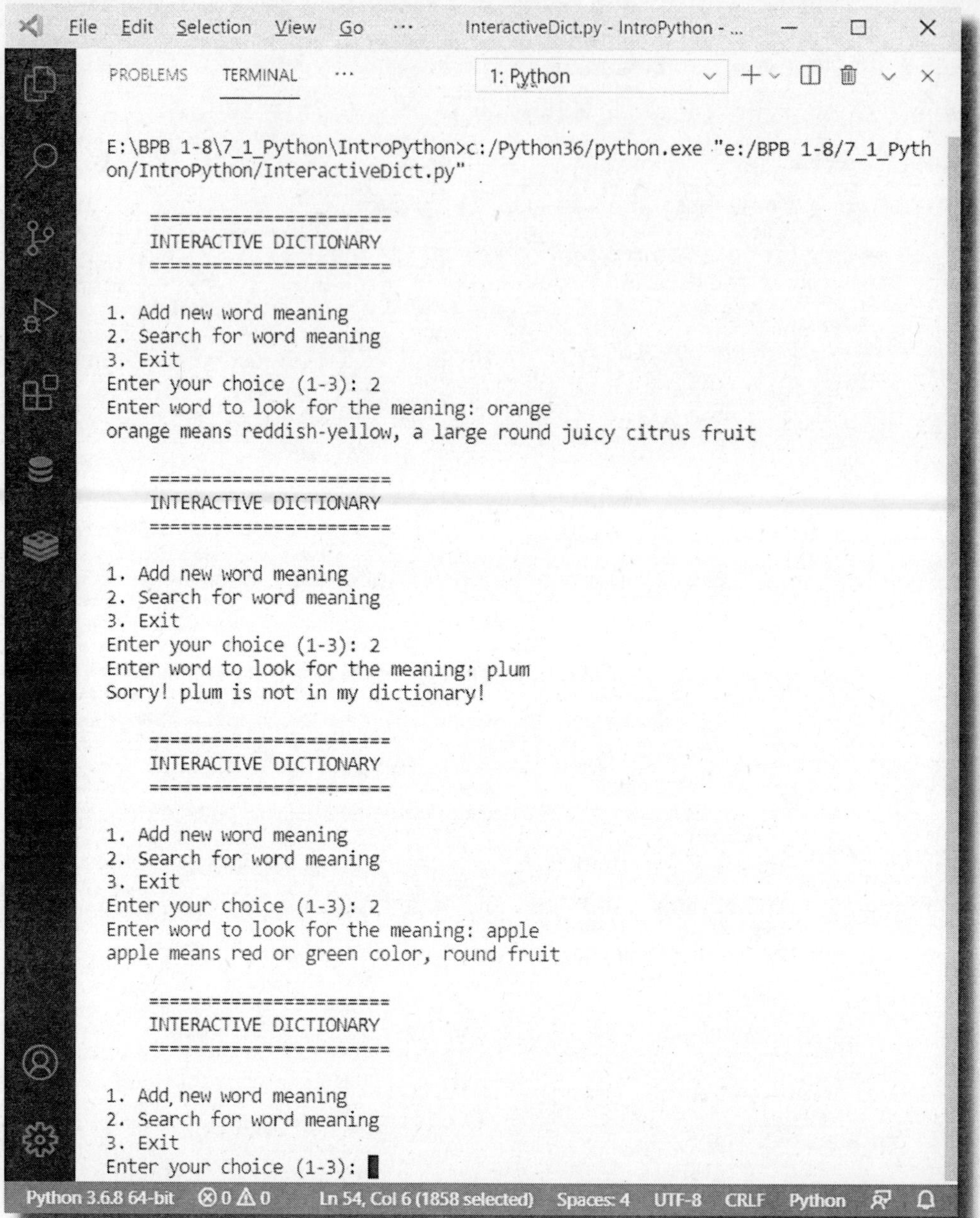

Figure 6.5(a): Output window for Interactive Dictionary

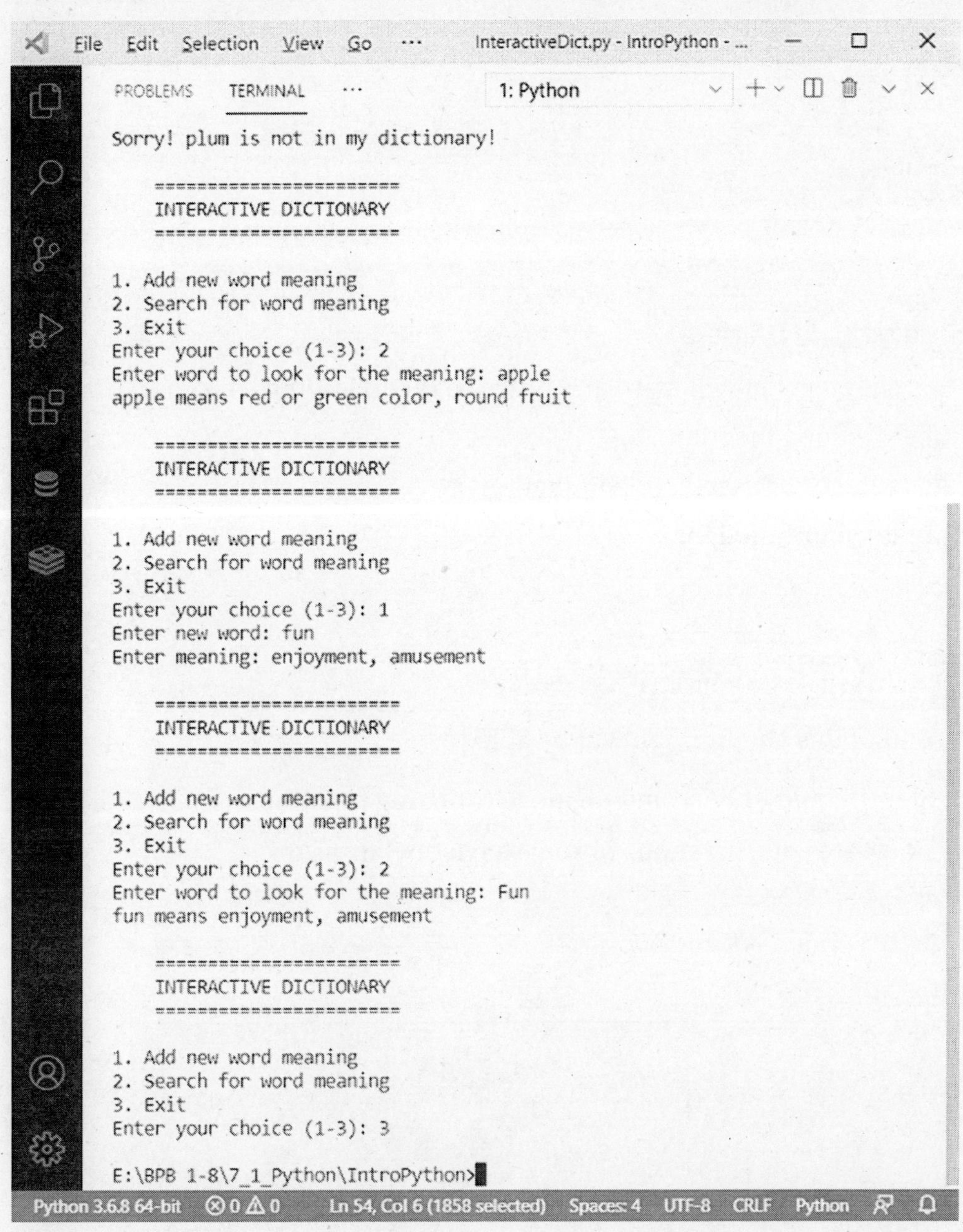

Figure 6.5(b): Output window for Interactive Dictionary

User-defined Functions

Structure

In this chapter, you will learn and practice the following concepts:

- User-defined function
- Advantages of user-defined functions
- Create your functions

Learning Objective

At the end of this chapter, you will be able to:

- Identify, and understand the need for using functions
- To create your functions to solve a particular task

PROJECT

Cryptography

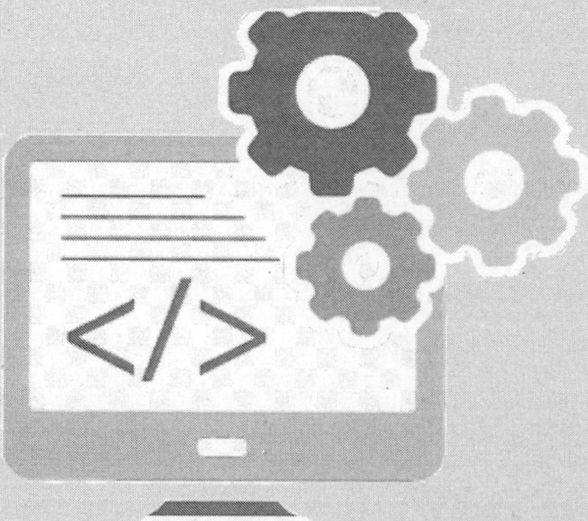

User-defined Functions

Functions that the programmer creates to solve a particular task is known as a **user-defined function**.

We create functions as it helps in the following ways:

- A repeated task can be written once and called as many times as we want.
- A large program will become smaller by reducing the length of the code.
- Debugging becomes easier.

Defining a function:

The keyword **def** is used to declare a function followed by the function name and parenthesis. The colon (:) at the end of the statement makes the block of the function be written to perform the task.

```
def function_name():
    FunctionBody
```

Activity 7.1

Create a function to display 'Welcome to the world of programming'.

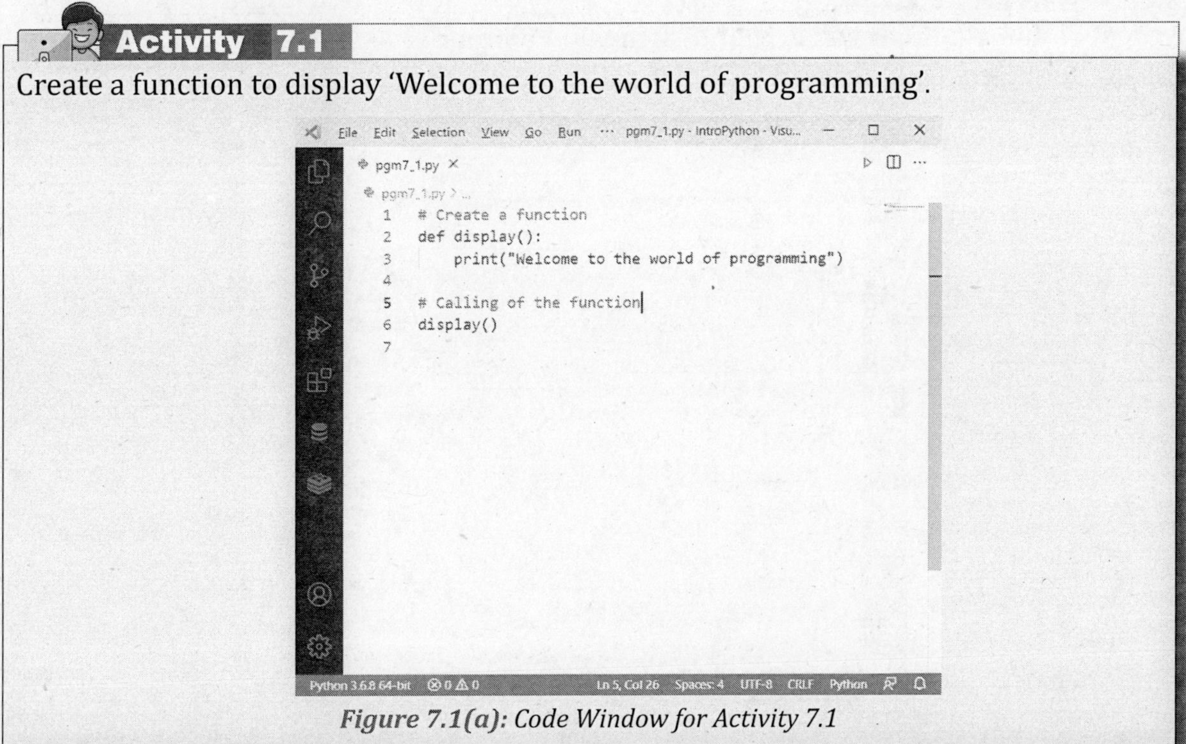

Figure 7.1(a): Code Window for Activity 7.1

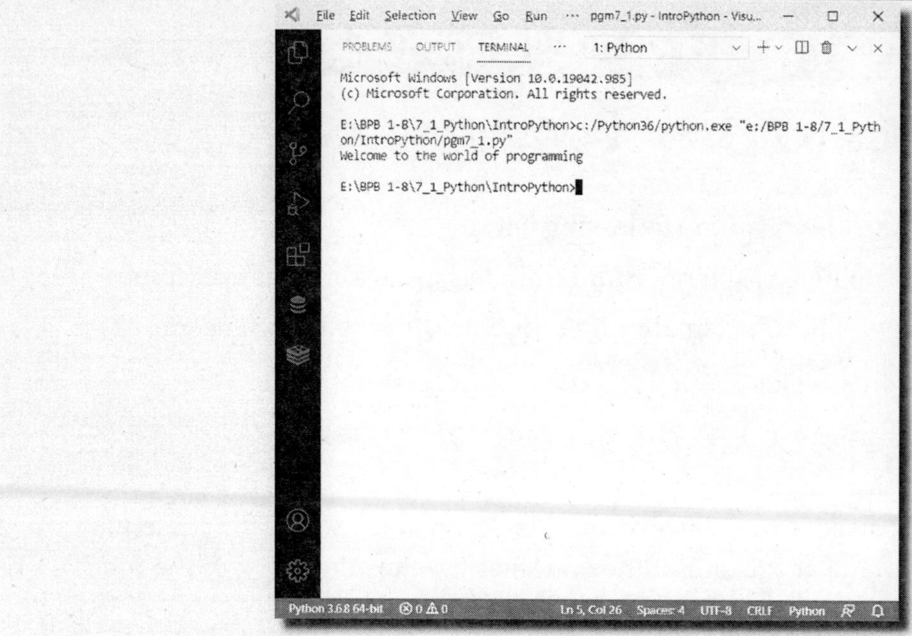

Figure 7.1(b): Output Window for Activity 7.1

Activity 7.2

Create a function that will accept a string and a number as two arguments, print the string and square of the number.

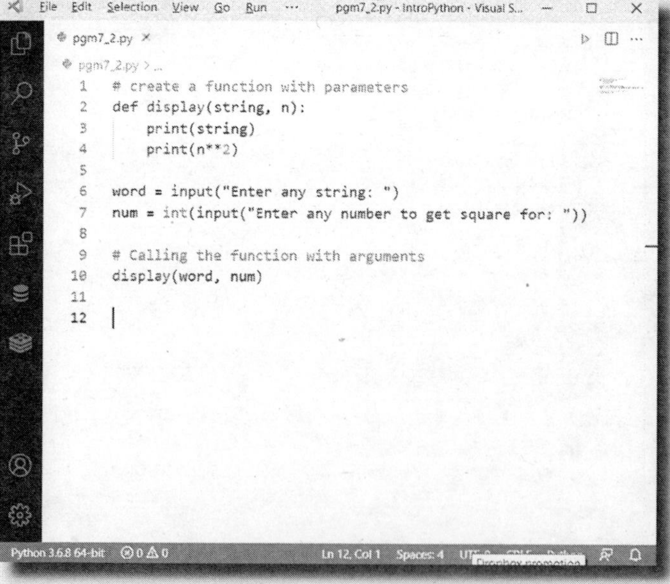

Figure 7.2(a): Code Window for Activity 7.2

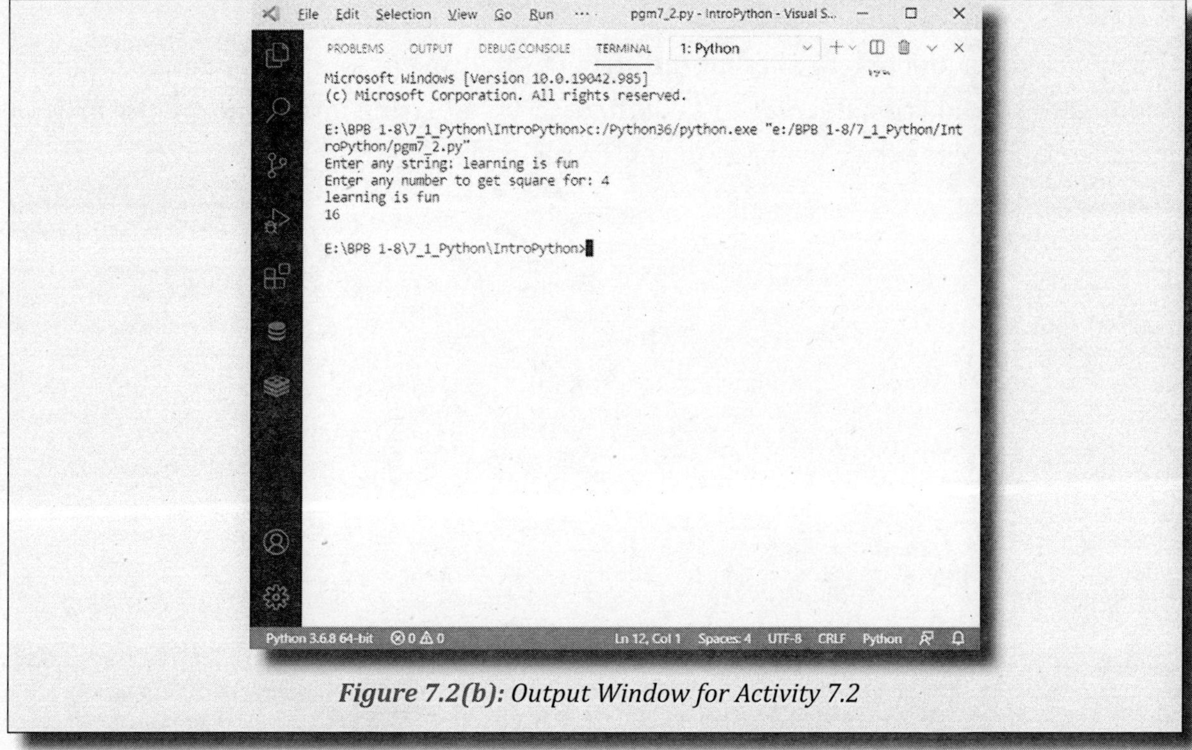

Figure 7.2(b): Output Window for Activity 7.2

Practice Questions:

- Create a function to calculate and display the multiplication table for the number passed as an argument to it.
- Create a function to accept a string and display the string in uppercase without using built-in functions.

Project

Cryptography

Cryptography means converting a message i.e., encode it to a secured message while sending and can be decoded at the receiver's end to read it.

Let us create a menu-driven code:

- Encrypt message
- Decrypt message

- Exit

We will create a function to encrypt the string by shifting letters to the defined number and create the function decrypt to take the encrypted string and generate the original message i.e., reverse the ciphertext to get the plain text.

```
# Cryptography

# list of letters to be used in encryption
letters = ['a', 'b', 'c', 'd', 'e', 'f', 'g', 'h', 'i', 'j', 'k', 'l', 'm', 'n',
         'o', 'p', 'q', 'r', 's', 't', 'u', 'v', 'w', 'x', 'y', 'z']
playing = ''

# function for encryption
def encrypt(str, n):
result = []
  # iterate over the string
  for x in str:
    # if space is encounterd then no change
    # it will be added in the list as space
    if x == " ":
      converted = " "
      result.append(converted)
    else:
      # As there are 26 letters
       #index of the letter will be added with the key and
      #then divide it by 26 and take remainder
      #to get the next character after that key
      converted = (letters.index(x) + n) % 26
      result.append(letters[converted])
  # convert the list into a string using join() function
  final = ''.join(result)
  print(final)
```

```
# function for decryption
def decrypt(str, n):
result = []
    # iterate over string
    for i in str:
        # space to be taken as space
        if i == " ":
            converted = " "
            result.append(converted)
        else:
            #reverse takeindex minus key& take the remainder
            converted = (letters.index(i) - n) % 26
            # converted character added to the list
            result.append(letters[converted])
    # list converted to string
    final = ''.join(result)
    print(final)

# Menu-driven code to keep in a loop till user enters quit
while playing != 'quit':
    #read text from user,convertinto lowercase before assigning
    text = input('Enter the text: ').lower()
    # read the key by which it has to be encrypted or decrypted
    key = int(input("Enter the key: "))
    #ask user to encrypt or decrypt and convert it also to lowercase
    choice = input('Do you want to encrypt or decrypt? ').lower()
    #encrypt function called with text and key
    if choice == 'encrypt':
        encrypt(text, key)
    #decrypt function will be called with the text and the key
    elif choice == 'decrypt':
```

```
        decrypt(text, key)
playing = input('Enter quit to stop: ')
```

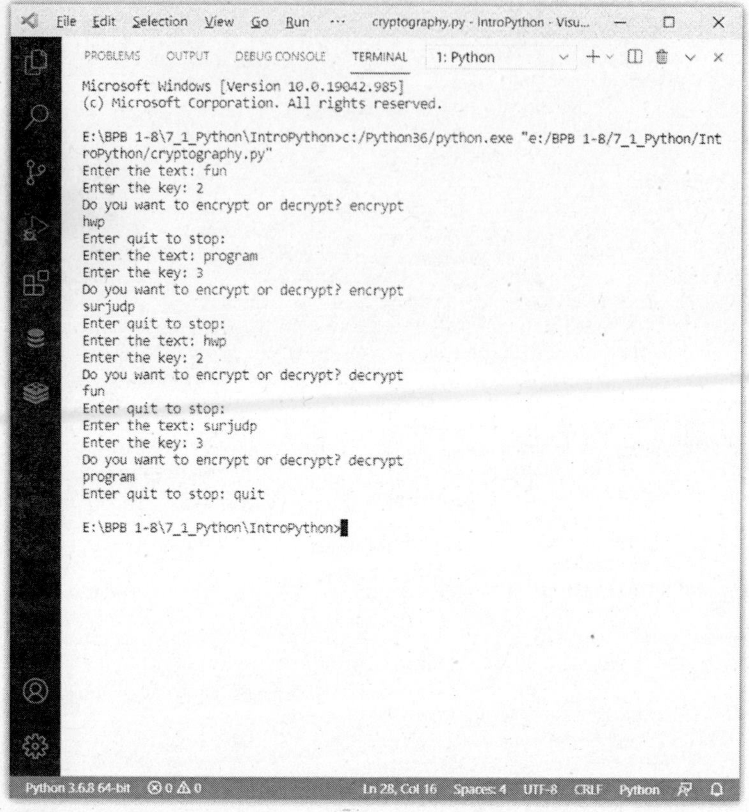

Figure 7.3: Output Window for Project Cryptography